Yes, Black Men Do Love Black Women!

An Empowerment Guide For Black Women

Coach Michael Taylor

Published by Creation Publishing Group LLC
www.creationpublishing.com

© 2024 Coach Michael Taylor

ISBN # 979-8-9857286-6-8

Library of Congress Number # 2024919477

Published and printed in the United States of America.

Table of Contents

Introduction

∞

$\mathcal{J}$n a world where media narratives and societal misconceptions often paint a distorted picture of Black love, this book stands as both a declaration and a celebration. "Yes, Black Men Do Love Black Women" isn't just a title—it's a truth that needs to be spoken, amplified, and understood. As a life coach and advocate for healthy relationships within our community, I've witnessed countless examples of deep, abiding love between Black men and women that rarely make headlines or social media trending topics.

The persistent narrative that Black men don't support or appreciate Black women has created unnecessary walls between us, fostering distrust and perpetuating cycles of hurt. This toxic storyline has seeped into our consciousness, affecting how we view ourselves and approach relationships. It's time to shatter this myth and reveal the fuller, more nuanced truth of Black love.

This book is born from countless conversations, coaching sessions, and observations of thriving Black relationships. It's designed to be more than just a rebuttal to negative stereotypes—it's a comprehensive guide to empowerment for Black women who deserve to experience the fullness of life and love. Within these pages, you'll find practical wisdom and strategic guidance for creating an extraordinary life built on five essential pillars:

1. Inner Peace: Discovering the power of self-love and emotional well-being
2. Dynamic Health: Nurturing your body and mind for optimal vitality
3. Great Relationships: Building and maintaining fulfilling connections, romantic and otherwise

4. Financial Abundance: Creating wealth and security on your own terms

5. Purpose and Meaning: Connecting with your divine calling and living intentionally

This book isn't about dependency or waiting for someone else to complete you. Instead, it's about recognizing your inherent worth, understanding that you are deeply loved and valued by Black men in your community, and using that knowledge as a foundation to create the extraordinary life you deserve.

The journey ahead is one of transformation, healing, and empowerment. It's about reclaiming narratives, rebuilding trust, and creating new possibilities for Black love and Black life. Whether you're single, dating, married, or focused on personal growth, this guide is designed to meet you where you are and help you get to where you want to be.

Let's begin this journey together, grounded in the truth that Black men do indeed love Black women, and empowered by the knowledge that an extraordinary life is not just possible—it's your birthright.

Welcome to your guide to empowerment, love, and abundance.

Coach Michael Taylor

Acknowledgements

I always begin each book I write by acknowledging the source of my creativity and passion. I choose to call this source **Divine Intelligence**. It is this Intelligence that fills me with hope, optimism, compassion, wisdom, and purpose. It is the source of my desire to help make the world a better place, and I am committed to working hand in hand with this Intelligence to help heal humanity. Some people might use the word God, but for me, **Divine Intelligence** feels more accurate.

So, to **Divine Intelligence**, I simply say, "Thank you!" Thank you for the unique gifts and talents you've given me, and I accept the responsibility of using those gifts to help create heaven on earth.

When it comes to Black women, I must begin by acknowledging the most amazing Black woman I know. My mom, Geneva, is the epitome of a strong Black woman. She is by far the most influential woman in my life, and everything I am is the result of the lessons I learned from her. My mom instilled in me a strong sense of self-identity, she taught me the value of a great work ethic, she instilled a sense of positivity and optimism in me, she taught me resilience and how to bounce back from any adversity, and she taught me the value of family first. She is a powerful, positive role model of the quintessential Black woman.

I love you, Mom!

I mentioned in my introduction that there is a misconception that Black men don't love and support Black women. There is also a misconception that Black women don't love and support Black men. It's important that we disrupt these misconceptions by showcasing and highlighting positive stories about Black love and how we really do love and support each other. With that being said, I must acknowledge the amazing Black woman I get to call my wife. My wife, Bedra, and I have been happily married for 23 years (together for 25). She is the most loving, supportive, and caring woman I have ever met. Not only does she accept me just as I am, she lovingly accepted my three children as her own, and she's the best bonus mom I could have ever wished for. She is my biggest cheerleader and promoter, and I count my blessings every day to have her as my life partner.

I love you, Mrs. B!

There is a very special group of women I must acknowledge. I put together an online event called the **Brotha to Sistah Empowerment Summit**. These 10 amazing Black women joined me to share their knowledge and wisdom to support Black women in creating extraordinary lives. I was blown away by their generosity in sharing their insights and strategies.

You can join the summit here: www.sistahsummit.com

Here is a list of these amazing women with the topics of their presentations and links to their websites and services:

- **Jewel Diamond Taylor** – Black Women Empowerment and Transformation www.jeweldiamondtaylor.com
- **Janine Ingram** – The Power of Self-Love www.janineaingram.com
- **Anita Charlot** – The Grown Ass Woman Philosophy www.anitacharlot.com

- **Anitra Rice** – Understanding and Healing From Grief and Loss www.thefolfoundation.org

- **Dr. Audrey Dawson** – Keys to Building a Healthy Blended Family ahinds2014@gmail.com

- **Dr. Candace Canady** – Your Body Is Your Temple www.coupleofchiros.com

- **Franka Baly** – Are You Ready to Become an Entrepreneur? www.fbuxconsulting.com

- **Dr. Omai Kofi** – Get Your Mind Right to Get Your Money Right www.meetdro.com

- **Dr. Pam Perry** – Building a Powerful Brand Identity www.pamperrypr.com

- **Rev. Bernette Jones** – Developing True Connection With the Divine www.consciousnessagency.com

Last but definitely not least, I'd like to acknowledge you, the reader, for taking the time to read this book. If you're the type of person who would read this type of book, it tells me that you are committed to living an extraordinary life. I'm absolutely certain it's not an accident that you're reading this book right now. There is a part of you that wants to create an extraordinary life, so pay attention to that still, small voice within that guided you to this book at this time, and know you have everything you need already inside you to build the life you know you deserve.

Good luck on your journey!

FOREWORD

∞

Jewel Diamond Taylor

Dear sistah!

*Y*ou will be glad you added this book to your personal library.

This book is for every Black woman who has ever questioned her worth, felt weighed down by expectations, or searched for a path to true peace and fulfillment. Within these pages, you'll find more than just words—you'll find reflections of your resilience, your grace, and your boundless capacity to thrive.

As you turn each page, know you are worthy of joy, abundance, and relationships that nourish your soul. This journey is about embracing every facet of your being, healing the wounds that have held you back, and reclaiming your power in every aspect of your life. You will be able to wipe your "lens" to see your possibilities for relationships wisdom, peace, financial freedom, and radiant health. This is your space to feel seen, valued, and uplifted.

Let this book be a guide, a companion, and a celebration of the unique and extraordinary woman that you are.

Stay in the light,

Dr. Jewel Diamond Taylor,

Keynote Speaker, author, The EmpowHERment Coach, Founder of Women on the Grow, Inc. 501(c)(3)

www.jeweldiamondtaylor.com

People of different religions and cultures live side-by-side
in almost every part of the world, and most of us have
overlapping identities which unite us in very different groups.

We can love what we are, without hating what- and who we
are not. We can thrive in our own tradition, even as we learn
from others, and come to respect their teachings"
— Kofi Annan

CHAPTER 1

Cultural Conditioning

In the world of personal development, one of the most profound realizations we can have is that our minds are shaped by the culture we live in. We absorb messages, often unconsciously, from various sources—media, family, education, and society at large. These messages influence how we view the world, how we see ourselves, and, most importantly, how we perceive others. For Black women, these perceptions have been molded by deeply ingrained stereotypes that have been perpetuated for centuries through media and societal narratives. To break free from these limitations, it's essential to examine the impact of cultural conditioning and the ways it affects how Black women are seen and treated.

Historically, the media has played a significant role in shaping public perception of Black women. Often, these portrayals have been harmful and limiting. Whether it's the "angry Black woman," the hypersexualized Jezebel, or the nurturing "mammy" figure, these tropes have been reinforced repeatedly, creating a one-dimensional view of Black women in the collective consciousness.

These stereotypes not only perpetuate negative behavior toward Black women but also diminish their humanity. They strip away the complexities of their experiences, reducing them to caricatures. These harmful images not only affect how others treat Black women but also seep into the consciousness of Black women themselves. They can internalize these stereotypes, limiting their potential and fueling self-doubt.

Racism and discrimination exacerbate this problem. They amplify the negative portrayals and dehumanize Black women, presenting them as less deserving of respect, success, and dignity. This perception often results in Black women being judged more harshly than others, both in the workplace and in everyday life. It can create a barrier to their personal and professional growth, as they are forced to navigate a world that does not fully see or appreciate their worth.

Racism is not just an individual act of hatred or prejudice; it's a system that infiltrates every aspect of life, shaping how people of color, particularly Black women, are viewed and treated. Discrimination, both overt and covert, arises from this system. Media outlets, for decades, have been influenced by racial hierarchies that prioritize and glorify certain types of beauty, success, and intelligence, all while relegating Black women to the margins.

These systems of racism and discrimination create a cycle. Stereotypes lead to biased portrayals, which fuel negative perceptions, which then justify continued mistreatment and underrepresentation. This conditioning causes people of all races, including Black women themselves, to unconsciously accept these narratives as truth. Over time, this perpetuates societal inequities and fosters a sense of inferiority in Black women, while leading others to view them through a distorted lens.

However, this doesn't have to be the reality. By recognizing the origins and effects of these stereotypes, we can break the cycle and challenge our conditioned beliefs. We can actively work toward a new, empowered understanding of Black women—one rooted in truth, dignity, and humanity.

The first step in dismantling cultural conditioning is to recognize it for what it is: a construct that doesn't serve us or the people we interact with. When we question the messages we've absorbed, we open ourselves to seeing Black women in their full complexity. We see their strength, resilience, creativity, intellect, and compassion—not as traits confined to a box, but as characteristics that are fluid and multifaceted.

To change perception, we must shift from viewing Black women as the sum of negative stereotypes to understanding them as individuals with unique stories, experiences, and strengths. Each Black woman carries a depth of history, culture, and personal power that goes far beyond what media portrayals suggest. Their contributions to society are vast, and their capacity for leadership, innovation, and influence is immense.

Moreover, it's crucial to acknowledge the trauma that racism and discrimination have caused, while also celebrating the triumphs Black women achieve despite these barriers. Black women have long been leaders, innovators, healers, and changemakers. They have weathered storms of injustice, not just for their own sake but for the benefit of future generations. Recognizing this legacy of resilience reframes the narrative from one of victimhood to one of strength and empowerment.

When we begin to shift our perception, something transformative happens—not only for Black women but for society as a whole. As people of all races come to understand and respect the fullness of Black womanhood, relationships improve, workplaces become more inclusive, and communities grow stronger. Seeing Black women in their full humanity enriches everyone's lives. It allows us to connect more deeply, with greater empathy, and move toward a society rooted in justice, equity, and love.

It is vital that we all play a role in this transformation. Whether through media, in personal conversations, or within our communities, we must challenge negative portrayals of Black women and demand more authentic and respectful representations. We must also support and uplift Black women, ensuring they have the space and opportunity to thrive without the weight of unjust expectations.

Black women are not bound by the limitations society imposes on them. By breaking free from the grip of cultural conditioning, they stand as symbols of strength, grace, and possibility. As we work to shift perceptions, let us be reminded that doing so is not just an act of liberation for Black women but a profound step toward the liberation of all humanity. When Black women rise, we all rise. Let this chapter be a reminder of the power of breaking free from stereotypes and embracing the brilliance and beauty of Black womanhood.

Here's my question to you, how do you, as a black woman, break free from the stereotypes and cultural conditioning in order to embrace your beauty and your brilliance?

The answer lies in your willingness to invest in your own personal growth and development, and reading books like this can provide you with the insights and wisdom to unlock your potential and become the best version of yourself. To become the best version of yourself, it is absolutely imperative that you fully understand who you are and why you are here.

So, are you ready to discover who you really are? I believe you are, so let's get started. I'm going to share an excerpt from my previous book titled *Adversity Is Your Greatest Ally.*

I would like you to take a moment to read the quote below:

"You are more than your thoughts, your body, or your feelings. You are a swirling vortex of limitless potential who is here to shake things up and create something new that the Universe has never seen."

As you read the quote, what thoughts came to mind? How did you feel after reading it? Did you feel excited? Scared? Confused? Uncertain? What if the quote is true? What if I told you that you are an unlimited being with infinite potential?

Would you believe me?

Unfortunately, most people wouldn't. But the fact that you are reading this book right now tells me that you are not "most people." If you are the type of person who reads a book like this, that tells me that you are open-minded, curious, and willing to learn and grow, and therefore, it's quite possible that you believe the quote. As a matter of fact, you've probably already agreed with it and are now ready to create something new that the Universe has never seen—so let's just jump right in and get started.

The truth is, there's an overwhelming majority of people who do not believe the quote. They will accept societally-driven labels that define who they are without ever asking themselves deeper questions like "Who am I, and why am I here?" This chapter is designed to give you some insights on possibly answering those two questions for yourself. Are you ready to answer those questions for yourself?

If you ask most people who they are, they will usually respond with answers such as their name, whether they have a family, what they do for a living, if they are a Democrat or Republican, an African American or Caucasian, a Christian or a Muslim (or part of a host of other religions), an American or Asian—the list of labels goes on and on. But if you think really deeply about this, these are just titles and labels that we use to try to define who we are. To prove my point, I want you to do a simple test. Walk up to a mirror and ask yourself what you see. Do you see a Republican? A Christian? A wife? A manager?

The answer is that you see a human being. The mirror can't lie; it can only reflect what is placed in front of it. All the titles and labels that you use to define yourself aren't who you are; they are simply titles, labels, and beliefs that you have accepted to define yourself. For example, have you ever known someone who used to be a Republican, but then became a Democrat? Or someone who was a Christian, who then became a Muslim? Or maybe someone who was pro-life, then became pro-choice? If they looked in the mirror as a Republican and then became a Democrat, what would they see in the mirror? They would see a human being, not a label. Labels are really just beliefs. You are not a label. You are a human being with different beliefs, and although your beliefs may change, you will not.

What you see in the mirror is what you truly are, but it goes a lot deeper than that. What you are is not necessarily who you are.

Who Are You?

Let me explain in more detail.

What you are is a human being with flesh and bones. This is an undisputable fact. But who you are is the divine being that resides within the flesh and bones. Here is another way to look at it—if I stand in front of a mirror and look at myself, I notice that I'm wearing a shirt. So, if I say that is "my" shirt, who owns it? I do—it is "my" shirt. Now, I continue to look into the mirror and notice my body. Who is the "me" that owns the body? If this is "my" body, who am I? I would like to suggest that the "me" that owns the body is actually my spirit. Put another way, you are not actually a human being having a spiritual experience—you are a spiritual being having a human experience, and your body is just like the suit of clothes that you are wearing.

If you can wrap your mind around this idea, then the original quote that I began this chapter with should make more sense to you. The quote said, "You are a swirling vortex of limitless potential who is here to shake things up and create something new that the Universe has never seen," which simply means that you are a divine spiritual being expressing yourself through human form. You have unique gifts and talents that must be shared with the world if you truly want to live a rewarding and fulfilling life.

So, what do you think? Do you believe this? Can you accept that you are much more than your physical body? Can you embrace the idea that you are a divine spiritual being with unlimited potential who is here to shake things up?

Since you're still reading this book, that means you're ready to dive deep into who you really are! So let's begin with understanding your divine makeup.

You are actually a three-part being, which can be described as body, mind, and spirit. You are a spirit, which is housed in a body that has a mind. Your body is like the clothes you are wearing, and your mind is like a tool that you use to help make conscious decisions and to learn new things. They all work in harmony.

As a spiritual being, you have an infinite capacity for learning and creativity. There are absolutely no limits to the number of things you can learn and create. You are only limited by your imagination, and even your imagination is unlimited.

So, let's break down the three parts of your being.

Let's begin with your mind.

It's important that you understand what your mind is and how it works if you truly want to discover who you really are. I'll begin by saying that the mind and the brain are not really the same thing. Your brain is the organ that serves as the center of your nervous system and is responsible for cognitive thinking and memory. In my opinion, it is the most amazing organ in your body, and it works just like a muscle—the more you use it, the stronger it gets.

The mind, however, is separate and distinct from the brain, although they work together. It is almost impossible to truly define the mind. Scientists have been trying to define it in scientific terms for millennia, but unfortunately, there has never been a consensus on exactly what the mind is. Rather than try to argue and define it, I will simply share a definition that I truly resonate with, and it is this definition I will use to explain what I believe the mind does and how it works.

The mind is "the element of a person that enables them to be aware of the world and their experiences, to think, and to feel; the faculty of consciousness and thought."

I really like the last part of this definition: "the faculty of consciousness and thought."

According to Dr. Bruce Lipton, author of the amazing book *The Biology Of Belief*, the mind actually has two parts: the conscious mind and the subconscious mind. A great metaphor to explain how it works is an iceberg. If you look at an iceberg in the ocean, you will only see a small portion of it above the water, but did you know that in some cases, 90% of the iceberg is actually below the surface? This is how the mind works. The top 10% is your conscious mind, and the lower 90% is your subconscious mind. What is really fascinating is that the subconscious mind is actually 1,000 times more powerful than the conscious mind when it comes to influencing your behavior.

Dr. Lipton explained it this way:

When we are born, we are completely conscious of all the external stimuli that we interact with. As children, we process primarily through our feelings without judgment or thought about the situation. In other words, we use our hearts, not our minds, to interpret everything around us. Our feelings become the guidepost of our experiences. During the first 7–10 years of our lives, our subconscious mind works like a video recorder. It simply records all the external events in our lives, and then it begins associating feelings, memories, and beliefs with those events. As we grow older, we begin to form subconscious beliefs about everything we come into contact with. As we form these beliefs, we then begin making assumptions about who we are and how we fit into the world.

Our prerecorded tapes become our subconscious beliefs about ourselves, and everything we think and do is then filtered through, and influenced by, these prerecorded tapes.

So take a moment to think about your own childhood, especially between the time when you were born and when you turned seven. What do you remember? Do you remember growing up in a loving, caring home, or was it one filled with violence and dysfunction?

Whether you realize it or not, your childhood has a strong impact on your behavior, even as an adult. If you remember being loved and nurtured as a child, the chances are your subconscious mind is filled with positive beliefs about yourself. In other words, your prerecorded tapes are positive, which in most cases means you will feel good about yourself and have a positive attitude about life. On the other hand, if you remember pain and misery growing up, there is a good chance that your prerecorded tapes about yourself may be negative, which in turn may cause you to create a negative outlook on life.

You can look at the subconscious mind as a big memory bank that stores your beliefs, memories, and life experiences. All your thoughts are instantly processed through your subconscious beliefs. Look at it this way: once your subconscious tapes are programmed during your childhood, every thought and action you have as an adult will be based on the programming you experienced growing up.

I'd like to take this time to share an example from my own life.

I was separated from my mom at the age of six, and I then created a subconscious belief that the people who love you will always leave you. As an adult, that may sound irrational, but as a six-year-old, my mother meant the world to me, and having her leave me was devastating and emotionally traumatizing.

As a result of this event, I created a subconscious belief that there was something wrong with me that caused my mother to leave. The primary belief I created was that I was unlovable. In order not to feel the shame and abandonment I experienced when my mother left, I created an unconscious strategy that I thought would keep me from feeling pain and also keep people in my life from leaving.

That strategy was for me to become a super nice guy in hopes of keeping people around that I cared about. By becoming a super nice guy, I put other people's emotional and psychological needs ahead of my own, and I was constantly trying to take care of others before taking care of myself. This is called co-dependence, and it was the reason I struggled with relationships earlier in my life.

I didn't realize it as I was growing up, but that single event laid the foundation of how I interacted in all of my relationships as an adult. My subconscious beliefs about myself actually sabotaged my relationships.

I would enter into a relationship where I would be the super nice guy. I would do all the right things that a woman would want in a relationship. I was attentive and respectful, and I had no problems showing affection. I had a great sense of humor and definitely believed in monogamy. On the surface, I appeared to be the perfect guy, but unfortunately, my subconscious beliefs about not being good enough and the deep-seated fear of abandonment kept me from being truly authentic in relationships, which kept me from experiencing true intimacy. No matter how much a woman loved me, that deep-rooted fear I had convinced me that something was wrong with me, which led to the fear that eventually the women in my life would leave.

Based on this subconscious fear, what do you think happened in my relationships? Of course, the women in my life would leave. I created an amazing pattern in all of my relationships, especially after my divorce. I would enter into a relationship, and it would last two to three weeks, and then the women would end up saying that they "cared too much" about me to stay in the relationship.

At the time, it made absolutely no sense to me that women would say that. How could you care about someone but, at the same time, leave them? After some deep self-introspection and emotional healing, I was able to recognize how my subconscious beliefs had been sabotaging my relationships, and I figured out how to break the pattern (I will explain how I did this in a later chapter).

The point I'm trying to make is how powerful the subconscious mind really is. Remember, the subconscious mind is separate and distinct from your brain—it is the faculty of consciousness and thought.

On the other hand, you have your conscious mind, which could be referred to as your "intellect." The conscious mind is where you store information that you have learned through rigorous study and learning. When you go to school and learn facts, you are using your conscious mind. When you calculate and figure out solutions to most problems, you are also using your conscious mind, but remember what I said about the subconscious mind being 1,000 times more powerful than the conscious mind?

Here is an example of how this works.

Imagine that you know someone who has a Ph.D. in astrophysics. This person is obviously extremely intelligent and has a highly developed conscious mind. But imagine, too, that this person has difficulty creating healthy relationships. No matter what they do, they always experience difficulty in relationships. Why do you think this is? They are obviously very smart, and yet they can't figure out how to make relationships work. Why is that?

Well, it's actually pretty simple. On a conscious level, they can read a book about relationships and explain to you intellectually how relationships work, which uses the conscious mind. But their subconscious is 1,000 times more powerful than their conscious mind, so when they enter into a relationship, the subconscious beliefs they have about themselves will always override the conscious mind. No matter how many books they read or how smart they are, if they have deeply rooted negative subconscious beliefs about themselves, they will never be able to create healthy relationships.

This is why it is so important to understand how the mind works. No matter how much we may learn on a conscious level, if we aren't willing to look at our subconscious beliefs, we can never truly change our lives. We each have deeply held subconscious beliefs about a wide variety of things, and until we become willing to change these subconscious beliefs, we will not be able to overcome our subconscious conditioning.

Let's take a look at some subconscious beliefs that may be sabotaging your life right now.

Are you currently struggling financially and can't figure out why? Well, there is a very good chance that your subconscious beliefs are actually keeping you from being financially secure. If you grew up hearing that money was the root of all evil or that rich people were stuck up and selfish, you may have subconscious beliefs that keep you from making a lot of money, because your subconscious belief might be that money is "bad."

If you're a man and you struggle with relationships, you may have subconscious beliefs that say women only want you for your money, or women can't be trusted. These beliefs will eventually sabotage any new relationship you enter. If you're a woman and you struggle with relationships, then it's quite possible that you have subconscious beliefs that say all men are dogs and only want sex. This belief will keep you from creating true intimacy with men because of your lack of trust. If you happen to be religious, you may have subconscious beliefs that you are a sinner and there is nothing you can do except repent of your sins and hope that God forgives you for being a sinner.

No matter what subconscious beliefs you have, you must understand that **they** are actually the cause of most of the pain, suffering, and lack of experience you have in life. To sum it up, your subconscious beliefs create your reality, so if you aren't happy with any area of your life right now, I can assure you that the main reason is that you have some unconscious belief that is causing you pain and misery.

Beliefs have long been understood as a core component of human identity. They shape how we perceive the world, how we interact with others, and, most importantly, how we view ourselves. For centuries, ancient spiritual teachings have posited that our thoughts have the power to influence the reality around us. This idea is encapsulated in expressions like "thoughts become things," found in diverse traditions, from Eastern philosophies to indigenous wisdom and even certain Western mystical traditions. Yet, it's only in recent decades that modern science, particularly quantum physics, has begun to provide a theoretical framework to support these ancient teachings.

The emerging understanding of the relationship between beliefs and reality is not only revolutionizing how we see the world but also confirming what spiritual teachers have claimed for millennia.

To understand how beliefs create reality, we must first understand what a belief is. Beliefs are more than just thoughts we consciously choose; they are deeply embedded mental constructs that influence our perception of everything we encounter. Beliefs form through repeated experiences, societal conditioning, and cultural narratives, becoming internal lenses through which we interpret events, people, and even our own potential.

Consider the placebo effect, one of the most well-documented phenomena in medicine. When patients believe they are receiving treatment, they often experience real physiological improvements—even when given an inert substance. This illustrates the profound influence belief has on our biology and our reality. If belief can induce healing in the body, could it not also affect other areas of life?

In fact, new scientific explorations suggest that beliefs do more than shape our inner world—they interact with the external world in ways we are only beginning to comprehend.

It is absolutely imperative that you begin examining your deeply held subconscious beliefs if you truly want to change, but rest assured that it is possible for you to do so. Throughout this book, I will be challenging you to examine your beliefs because the only way to truly change your life is to change your beliefs about it.

Now that you have a deeper understanding of how the subconscious mind works, here's the really good news: when you realize just how powerful the mind really is, you can use it to create anything you want in life.

Have you ever heard this quote: "Whatever the mind can conceive, you can achieve, if you really believe"?

Do you believe it? Is it really possible?

I believe the answer is "yes," and now I would like to share how and why this is possible. So let's go back to the definition I posted earlier: The mind is "the element of a person that enables them to be aware of the world and their experiences, to think, and to feel; the faculty of consciousness and thought."

I would like you to focus on "the faculty of consciousness and thought."

Here is another way to look at it. Try to imagine there is a Divine Intelligence that permeates the Universe. This Intelligence is actually the Source of all things. It is inherent in all things. It is what keeps the planets aligned and what causes a seed to grow into a flower. It is the same intelligence that causes a bone to heal and the Earth to orbit the sun.

There are lots of different names for this Source, but the name does not matter. You can call it God, The Creator, Yahweh, Jehovah, Great Spirit, The Universe, or any other name, but what is most important is that you believe and trust that it is available to you. Throughout this book, I will simply refer to it as The Source. You do not have to believe in any particular religion or dogma to have access to it; you must simply open your heart and your mind to the truth that it exists. If you accept this truth, then you must accept that your mind is actually connected to The Source. Your mind is like a conduit through which The Source allows divine intelligence to flow to you and through you. If you're familiar with the teachings of Jesus, the only prerequisite he gave to creating miracles was to believe they were possible. He then acknowledged that his Father was the source of the miracles.

Now you must remember what I said at the beginning: The mind and the brain are not the same thing. The brain can only process information that you have provided to it. The brain is not creative—it is not the source of imagination, creativity, or divine ideas. The brain is also not the source of inspiration or insight; these are all functions of the mind, which can also be referred to as the heart, or the center of your being.

Author and spiritual teacher Iyanla Vanzant said, "The mind is a powerful, creative energy. Everything we think, do, and feel begins in the mind. For this reason, we have to address the thoughts, beliefs, judgments, learnings, and perceptions that we hold in our minds."

The reason the quote "whatever the mind can conceive you can achieve" is true is because The Source of all things is purely creative and it needs you to co-create with it. So when your mind conceives a divine idea from The Source, which is all-powerful and limitless, you can accomplish it if you're willing to work hand-in-hand with The Source and put forth a whole lot of effort to bring it to fruition.

One of my favorite spiritual teachers is Deepak Chopra. He shared a very powerful quote that really speaks to this truth. He said: "Inherent in every intention and desire are the mechanics for its fulfillment." Put another way, The Source will not give you an idea that you can't accomplish. The Source knows exactly what you're capable of and will, therefore, only give you divine ideas that are attainable for you. You wouldn't even have the idea in the first place if you weren't capable of accomplishing it.

As I mentioned previously, the mind is the source of imagination, and therefore it is the key to creating anything you want in life. Let me share a brief story with you to validate my point.

During the darkest period of my life, I was deeply depressed and unsure of how I was ever going to get my life back on track. At the time, I had no money, no job, no relationship, no material possessions, and things seemed pretty hopeless. But the one thing I did have was my imagination, and I began to use it to help me change my situation. Despite that I had absolutely nothing, I began imagining my life getting better. Instead of focusing on all the things I didn't have, I focused my attention on what I did have. I would begin each day counting my blessings for everything that I had, such as my health, my ability to learn, my positive attitude, a few close friends, children who loved me, and the fact that I was even alive.

I began envisioning what my life would be like once I got back on my feet, and I somehow knew that eventually I would. As I continued to focus on the things that I did have and on the future that I wanted to create, things slowly started to change for me. Eventually, I found a job, then I purchased a car, and finally, I was able to get my own apartment. Although this took a couple of years, my point is that I used my imagination to see the things I wanted, and then I worked really hard to get them. It all began in my mind. I had to be willing to use my mind and imagination first before I could create the things I wanted.

As I think back in retrospect, I can now see how The Source was actually the source of all of the ideas that I used to put my life back together. It was The Source that would provide me with ideas on where to look for employment and that gave me the inspiration to remain positive even when I had nothing. It was The Source that gave me the strength and courage to move through all of my life's challenges without giving up and falling victim to despair. It was The Source that encouraged me and helped me to focus on my ultimate destiny, and it didn't allow me to quit.

Even through those difficult times, I held on to my dreams of one day being a successful entrepreneur, writer, and speaker. I had no evidence that I could do these things; I only had the belief and faith that I could. Belief and faith originate in the mind, and I now recognize that each of these originates from The Source.

And now here I am, some twenty years later, doing exactly what I imagined I would be doing—all because I chose to believe that whatever the mind can conceive, you can achieve.

It's important that you understand I am no different than you are. I am a divine spiritual being with direct access to The Source, and so are you. You have a mind and direct access to The Source. There is nothing you cannot accomplish if you choose to access your divinity, but it is up to you to go a little deeper and figure out what negative subconscious beliefs you may have about yourself and change them. It is only through this process of self-examination and change that you can truly live the life you were destined to live.

So, now let's talk about your body.

It is my belief that the most amazing thing on this planet is the human body. I do not believe that there is anything more miraculous. Although most people take their bodies for granted, I believe it is the greatest gift that The Source provided us with. I mentioned earlier that the body is simply a suit of clothing that your spirit wears, so I must admit that The Source knew exactly what it was doing when it created the human body.

Of course, everyone is aware of their own physical body, but did you know that you also have an emotional or energetic body?

If you accept the fact that you are a spiritual being, then it makes it easier to grasp how the emotional/energetic body works.

Think of it this way:

Imagine that you have an opening in the top of your skull, and there is a pipe that goes from the top of your skull to the bottom of your belly. This pipe flows with energy that comes directly from The Source; this energy is your life force, and it permeates your entire being. When you are born, the pipe is completely open, and it allows Source energy to flow through you easily. This energy causes you to feel alive and connected to life. This energy is then converted into feelings, which is the spirit's way of communicating with the body. There are primarily four energies that move throughout the energetic body: joy, anger, sadness, and fear.

As a child, whenever you experienced one of these feelings, you acted appropriately and expressed the feeling through an emotion. For example, if you felt sad, you would cry; if you felt angry, you would scream or lash out; if you felt joy, you would smile and laugh; and if you felt fear, you would close off or retreat. As long as you expressed the feeling appropriately, then the energetic pipe stayed open and clear, and your life force energy continued to flow through you.

As you grow older, your parents or family members begin conditioning you to believe that expressing emotions was wrong. What happens is you begin to repress and suppress your feelings, and each time you do, you create little energy blocks in the pipe. It's like building up plaque in your arteries. The more you suppress your feelings, the more the energetic pipe clogs up, and before you know it, the pipe is completely closed, and you are cut off from your life force. When this happens, you lose your sense of aliveness because the divine flow of energy has been cut off. Once the flow of energy has been cut off and we have been disconnected from The Source, we then learn to process everything through our conscious mind or intellect, and we become very rational and analytical. In other words, we try to rely on our brains instead of our hearts and minds.

The bad news is that the energetic body works like the subconscious mind. We may not be aware of it, but our repressed emotions cause us to act out irrationally sometimes because we are completely unconscious of the pain we may be carrying. Here is a good example: Have you ever met or known someone who is always angry? No matter what is going on, this person is angry and negative, and they usually aren't pleasant to be around. They get angry and upset at the slightest provocation, and no matter what you say or do, they will have a negative response to just about everything. Do you know anyone like that? Are you like that?

Why do you think this person acts this way? It's because they have trapped emotional energy in their emotional body, and until they learn how to release it, they will always act out of anger.

On the flip side of that, maybe you know someone who always pretends to be happy. They are the "people-pleasing" types that always seek approval, and they pretend that everything is always okay. The only emotion they express is happiness, but unfortunately, they are completely sad and emotionally bankrupt inside. A person like this usually has trapped anger, fear, or sadness in their emotional bodies, and rather than feel these emotions, they hide behind being happy all the time.

When we have repressed or suppressed emotions, they can sabotage all areas of our lives. As long as we feel and release our feelings appropriately, the life force can move through us. But as we shut down the flow, we create a disconnection from The Source, and it leads to all sorts of problems in our lives.

It's important that you take care of both your bodies—your physical body and your emotional one. You take care of the physical body by eating the right foods and exercising, and you take care of the emotional body by investing in some emotional healing work that allows you to release any repressed energy that is trapped in your emotional body. I will share some tips on how to do this in an upcoming chapter.

Now that you have a better understanding of how the mind and the body work together, it's time to fully understand who you really are.

Every major religion promotes a very simple and profound truth: There is a Source through which all things are created. It does not matter which religion you follow, as long as you accept this simple fact. This Source is the Divine Intelligence that created and is still creating the amazing Universe we live in, and you have unlimited access to this Source. As a human being, you are a divine expression of this Source, which means that you can co-create anything your heart desires with this Source.

Think of it this way: If you look at the ocean, you will see a powerful, beautiful, and seemingly infinite body of water. If you walk up to the ocean and scoop up a small cup of it, what you will have in the cup is ocean. This expression is no different than the ocean; as a matter of fact, it contains all of the same qualities, characteristics, and attributes of the ocean. In fact, it is the ocean in an individualized expression. As long as the expression of the ocean stays connected to the ocean, it will thrive and express exactly the way the ocean does. But the cup of ocean could never be the ocean in its totality, so therefore, it is a divine, individual expression of the ocean.

The Source is just like the ocean. You are an individual expression of The Source. You have all of the same qualities, characteristics, and attributes as The Source. You are no different than The Source. As long as you stay connected to The Source, you can co-create with it, and since The Source is infinite, so are you.

Do not buy into societal labels and constructs that will convince you that there is something wrong with you. Disregard all labels and titles, and come to the understanding that you are a divine spiritual being with unlimited potential, and the only thing that can keep you from accomplishing anything is yourself. This includes letting go of your attachment to your ethnic identity. You should definitely be proud of your ethnic heritage, whatever it may be, but you must understand that your spiritual nature has nothing to do with skin color or nationality. The Source transcends race, and therefore so do you if you choose to accept who and what you truly are.

Titles and labels will only hold you back, but accepting the truth of your being will definitely set you free. Remember that you are a three-part being—Spirit, Mind, and Body—that is connected to The Source, and you can, therefore, co-create anything your heart desires.

I would like to close this chapter with something for you to think about.

I would like for you to think about a snowflake.

If you look at snowflakes falling from the sky, it appears that they are all the same. They all have the same color, texture, and smell. They are all composed of the same stuff, and they all come from the same source. But if you look under a microscope, every snowflake is completely different. No two snowflakes are alike. Just imagine—out of the billions of snowflakes that fall from the sky, none of them are the same.

The truth is, you are just like the snowflake. Out of the 7 billion human beings on the planet, there is only one you. When it comes to human beings, The Source never replicates itself. You are a divine, unique individual expression of

The Source, and it is your responsibility to accept this fact.

Your job is to come to this understanding and recognize that you have unlimited potential, and you have been given some unique gifts and talents that are yours alone—and your job is to share them with the world. This is the reason that the quote I shared at the beginning of this chapter is so important. It states a divine truth, and I hope that you will take it to heart and accept it as your truth.

So I will leave you with that quote, and I hope that you will embrace it and accept the truth that it shares.

"You are more than your thoughts, your body, or your feelings. You are a swirling vortex of limitless potential who is here to shake things up and create something new that the Universe has never seen."

—Dr. Richard Bartlett

"When I dare to be powerful, to use my strength in the service of my vision, then it becomes less and less important whether I am afraid"
— Audre Lorde

CHAPTER 2

Black Women Are Amazing

To begin a chapter about Black women being amazing, I must start by acknowledging the most amazing Black woman I know: my mom, Geneva. As I reflect back over my life and reminisce about the challenges and obstacles she overcame, I am in absolute awe of just how amazing my mom truly is.

My mom was a single mother with six children back in the '60s. We were basically the poster children for poverty back then. From a very young age, I remember my mom working 2-3 jobs all the time just to make ends meet. Although we were poor, she never complained about it or acted like a victim of society. She always maintained a positive attitude, and she instilled in me the idea that, despite our circumstances, she still believed it was possible for anyone to live the American dream. I'll never forget one of the most powerful lessons she taught me when I was about 15 years old: "If you want something badly enough, there is no one, or nothing, that can keep you from attaining it except yourself!" That lesson became my mantra, and I attribute most of my success to accepting and believing it was true.

When I was six years old, my oldest sister was diagnosed with a brain tumor. This definitely put an emotional and financial strain on my mom. In order to deal with this, my mom decided to take me, along with one of my sisters and brothers, to live with our father. It was obviously a difficult choice, but it was one she had to make. For seven years, my mom dealt with my sister's illness, and eventually, she pulled through. After those seven years, I was reunited with my mom.

During my teenage and young adult years, my mother had to deal with a wide variety of personal challenges. We were living in government housing, and she was occasionally working 2-3 jobs to make ends meet. Despite those challenges, one of my fondest memories of her was when she took on an additional part-time job to pay for a tuxedo for me to go to my junior high prom. Although she must have been completely exhausted, I'll never forget the look on her face when I put on that tuxedo. She was beaming with pride, and I could feel her unconditional love for her son. This is just one example of the sacrifices my mom made for me, and it warms my heart every time I think about it.

When I was 18, I got a job and moved into my first apartment. My mother had instilled a strong work ethic in me, and it paid off handsomely as I climbed the corporate ladder and eventually became a manager for a multimillion-dollar building supply center.

After I moved out, my mother still faced a multitude of challenges. She became a widow twice and never remarried, and my sister, who suffered from the brain tumor, eventually passed away. Despite these difficulties, she maintained a positive attitude, and today, at 87 years young, she is happily single, healthy, and enjoying her life. At 85 years old, she even went on a hot air balloon ride with my daughter.

This is just a small snapshot of her life and the obstacles she had to overcome. Her story is one of faith, perseverance, resilience, determination, dedication, and hard work. These are the traits and qualities of most Black women, and it is the reason I titled this chapter: Black Women Are Amazing, because they truly are!

Since the intention of this book is to empower Black women, I would like to shed light on some things that might keep them from being amazing. In the first chapter, I talked about cultural conditioning and how the media shapes our beliefs and perceptions. It's important to be aware of some of the negative stereotypes and misrepresentations of Black women perpetuated by mainstream media.

Here is a list of 10 of the most pervasive negative stereotypes about Black women in America

1. The Angry Black Woman – A pervasive stereotype portraying Black women as hostile, aggressive, and confrontational, often used to dismiss their valid emotions or opinions.

2. The Strong Black Woman – While resilience is admirable, this stereotype suggests that Black women are invulnerable and don't need support or empathy, leading to their struggles being overlooked.

3. The Hypersexualized Jezebel – This stereotype reduces Black women to sexual objects, portraying them as overly promiscuous or lustful, rooted in historical narratives used to justify exploitation.

4. The Mammy Figure – A stereotype depicting Black women as selfless, nurturing caretakers who are only valued for their ability to serve others, particularly white families.

5. The Welfare Queen – A harmful stereotype portraying Black women as lazy, irresponsible, and dependent on government assistance, contributing to societal stigmas around poverty and welfare.

6. The Sapphire – A stereotype similar to the angry Black woman, but specifically depicting Black women as emasculating, domineering, and controlling, especially towards Black men.

7. The Overly Masculine Woman – This stereotype portrays Black women as lacking femininity, often associated with physical strength or assertiveness, and used to deny them traditional gender roles or beauty standards.

8. The Uneducated or Ignorant Woman – Black women are often misrepresented as intellectually inferior or lacking ambition, perpetuating the myth that they are less capable or less deserving of academic and professional success.

9. The Absent or Bad Mother – This stereotype unjustly portrays

Black women as neglectful or unfit mothers, reinforcing negative ideas about Black family dynamics and single parenthood.

10. The Exotic Other – Black women are often exoticized and portrayed as different, foreign, or mysterious, which dehumanizes them and reduces their identity to being "other" rather than individuals with diverse, complex experiences.

These stereotypes contribute to the dehumanization and marginalization of Black women, ignoring their true diversity and experiences, so it is important for you to recognize them and make sure you aren't acting consistent with any of them.

Overcoming negative media-generated stereotypes requires a conscious effort to reject limiting narratives and embrace a more empowering self-image. Start by recognizing that these stereotypes are often inaccurate, rooted in ignorance, and designed to perpetuate harmful biases. It's crucial to actively seek out positive representations in media, books, and communities that celebrate diversity and highlight success stories. Surround yourself with individuals who uplift and support your growth, and engage in conversations that challenge the status quo. By focusing on personal development, education, and cultivating self-worth, you can rise above the negativity and create your own narrative, free from the constraints of societal stereotypes.

Black women in America have long faced negative stereotypes that attempt to diminish their worth and capabilities, yet they continue to rise and succeed in extraordinary ways. Black women can and do achieve greatness. By cultivating self-love, harnessing their power, and building strong support networks, they rewrite the narrative, becoming beacons of success and empowerment for future generations.

In order to dispel negative stereotypes, it's important to acknowledge the facts that refute said stereotypes. Here is a brief list of facts that shatters the stereotypes and confirms how amazing black women really are:

1. Black women are the fastest-growing group of entrepreneurs: Between 2014 and 2019, the number of businesses owned by Black women grew by 50%, representing the fastest growth rate among all racial and ethnic groups. Black women own 2.7 million businesses, accounting for 21% of all women-owned businesses in the U.S. (American Express, 2019).

2. Increasing college graduation rates: Black women are the most educated demographic in the U.S. in terms of the number of associate and bachelor's degrees earned. More than 25% of Black women ages 25 and older hold a bachelor's degree or higher, a figure that has more than doubled since 2000 (U.S. Census Bureau, 2020).

3. Representation in politics: Black women have made historic gains in U.S. politics. In 2020, Vice President Kamala Harris became the first Black woman and woman of South Asian descent to hold the office of Vice President, a significant milestone for Black women in leadership. She is currently running to become the first female to hold the highest office in the nation as she runs to become the President of the United States. In 2022, Ketanji Brown Jackson became the first black woman to serve on the Supreme Court of the United States

4. Influence in corporate leadership: As of 2023, there are five Black women leading Fortune 500 companies as CEOs, a record number. This is a significant increase from zero in 2019, highlighting the growing presence of Black women in corporate boardrooms (Fortune, 2023).

5. STEM advancements: Black women in STEM fields are increasing in visibility and impact. Between 2017 and 2021, there was a 7.5% increase in the number of Black women earning degrees in STEM disciplines, showing their rising influence in traditionally underrepresented fields (National Center for Education Statistics, 2022).

6. Political representation growth: Black women currently hold more than 130 elected positions at the federal, state, and local levels, representing a dramatic increase over the past decade. This rise is pivotal in shaping policies and legislation that affect their communities (Higher Heights Leadership Fund, 2022).

7. Media and entertainment leadership: Black women are making significant strides in media ownership. For example, in 2021, Oprah Winfrey became the first Black woman to own a major cable network (OWN) and continues to be one of the most influential media moguls in the world (Forbes, 2022).

8. Military leadership: In 2021, Lieutenant General Nadja West became the first Black woman to serve as the Army Surgeon General and the highest-ranking Black female general in the U.S. Army, setting a powerful precedent for Black women in military leadership roles (U.S. Army, 2021).

9. Black women as a political force: In the 2020 election, Black women had the highest voter turnout rate of any demographic group, with over 90% of Black women casting their votes. Their political engagement played a crucial role in the outcomes of key races, including the election of President Biden and Vice President Harris (Pew Research Center, 2021).

10. Professional sports achievements: Black women are breaking barriers in sports leadership. In 2020, Kimberly Ng became the first woman and first Asian American general manager in Major League Baseball history, and a number of Black women have continued to dominate as coaches and executives in professional sports (MLB.com, 2020).

These statistics represent significant progress while acknowledging that barriers and disparities still exist. Black women continue to break new ground across various sectors of American society.

Black women have always been at the forefront of progress, resilience, and excellence in America. Despite the systemic barriers and societal limitations imposed on them, they continue to rise, showing us what true power, persistence, and perseverance look like. One cannot speak about the brilliance of Black women without acknowledging the challenges they've faced in a country where racism and sexism have often tried to block their paths to success. But it's precisely those obstacles that make their achievements even more inspiring.

At the heart of this conversation is Vice President Kamala Harris. As the first Black woman and South Asian woman to hold the office of Vice President of the United States, she shattered one of the highest glass ceilings in American politics. Her historic election was a moment of celebration not just for her but for all Black women who have dared to dream beyond the limitations society tried to place on them. Kamala's journey has not been easy. Born to immigrant parents, she learned early in life the value of hard work, resilience, and the importance of standing firm in her identity as a Black woman. She once said, "My mother would look at me and she'd say, 'Kamala, you may be the first to do many things, but make sure you're not the last.'" These words have fueled her persistence to rise above discrimination, stereotypes, and doubt. Her achievements are a testament to the brilliance and tenacity of Black women everywhere. Currently, she is seeking the highest office in the nation as she pursues becoming the first female president in the history of the United States of America.

Kamala Harris is just one of many examples. Across industries, Black women have consistently shown the world their greatness. From the boardrooms of Fortune 500 companies to the courts of the WNBA, from the classrooms of prestigious universities to the stages of award-winning performances, Black women are making their mark. Oprah Winfrey, one of the most successful media moguls in history, built an empire from scratch, becoming a global icon of leadership, philanthropy, and empowerment.

Beyoncé Knowles-Carter, an artist who has redefined what it means to be a cultural force, has used her platform to celebrate Black womanhood unapologetically. Both women have faced their fair share of struggles, but their resilience allowed them to turn obstacles into opportunities.

The obstacles that Black women face in America are not new. From the brutal legacies of slavery and segregation to the pervasive realities of wage gaps, underrepresentation, and stereotypes, Black women have always had to fight for their rightful place in society. In the workforce, Black women are often underpaid and underpromoted compared to their white counterparts, yet they remain among the fastest-growing groups of entrepreneurs in America. Their drive to create, innovate, and succeed is fueled not by external validation, but by an inner knowing that they are worthy of success.

This tenacity comes from a deep well of faith and resilience. Faith has always been a cornerstone for Black women. For generations, Black women have leaned on their spiritual practices to navigate the difficult terrains of life. Whether it's the hymns of a church choir, the wisdom passed down from elders, or the personal meditations that sustain them through hardship, faith has been a crucial component of their perseverance. It has kept Black women grounded, hopeful, and determined even when the odds were against them.

Take, for example, Shirley Chisholm, the first Black woman elected to Congress and the first to run for President under a major party. Her mantra, "Unbought and Unbossed," was not just a slogan; it was a declaration of her unwillingness to be constrained by the prejudices of her time. She faced racial and gender discrimination head-on but never let it deter her from her mission of justice and equality. Like so many Black women, her path was filled with obstacles, but her legacy stands as a beacon of what is possible when resilience and faith are combined with action.

And let us not forget the everyday Black women—mothers, daughters, sisters, and community leaders—who, despite facing racial and gender-based violence, economic inequality, and societal marginalization, continue to pour into their families, their communities, and their careers. These women, often unseen and underappreciated, embody the spirit of excellence that permeates Black womanhood. Their sacrifices, determination, and love continue to uplift the entire Black community.

Black women have shown that no matter the obstacle, they have the power to persevere. Their stories are stories of triumph, not because their challenges were less, but because their resolve was greater. From fighting for the right to vote to leading social justice movements, Black women have been the backbone of progress in this country. Their resilience, persistence, and perseverance serve as an inspiration to us all.

To every Black woman reading this, remember that you are part of a lineage of greatness. Your existence is proof that you are enough—just as you are. You have the power to create change, to shape the future, and to build a legacy that will inspire generations to come. And most importantly, know that you are loved, respected, and valued. You are awesome.

In the words of Vice President Kamala Harris: "You are powerful, and your voice matters. You're going to walk into many rooms in your life and career where you may be the only one who looks like you or has had your experiences. But remember, every time you break barriers, you make space for others to follow."

I'm convinced that we Black women possess a special indestructible strength that allows us to not only get down, but to get up, to get through, and to get over.
— Janet Jackson

CHAPTER 3

∞

Healing and Transformation

ack in the early '90s, I was walking through a grocery store when I noticed this very attractive woman looking at a box of cereal. She was reading the back of the box and then noticed I was looking at her. She put the box down and started walking towards me. As she walked past me, she smiled and said, "Nice mustache," as she continued to walk away. I turned around to follow her, and when I caught up to her, I asked shyly, "Were you talking to me?" "Of course, I was! You were the only person on the aisle." "Well, that was a pretty smooth pick-up line," I said. "It wasn't a pick-up line; it was simply an observation. You have a very nice mustache."

After chatting for several minutes, I asked her for her phone number and if she would like to go out with me. She said yes, and I said I would give her a call later so we could schedule a date.

I had been single for a few years and was now ready to start dating again. .

On our first date, it turned out we had a lot in common. We were both single parents, and both of us had been divorced for a few years. We enjoyed the same types of music, had the same philosophy about spirituality, enjoyed many of the same foods, and even read a lot of the same books. Hanging out with her was a lot of fun, and I really enjoyed being with her.

After a couple of months, we spent our first night together, and it turned out we were definitely sexually compatible. After approximately six months, I started having deep feelings for her, and I began to believe she might be the person I could spend the rest of my life with.

After approximately a year, I knew I was in love with her, and I asked her to marry me. At the time, I was just beginning my speaking and writing career. She was extremely supportive and encouraged me to pursue my dream of becoming an author and motivational speaker. We decided to move in together and began planning our future.

For the first few weeks, things were great. We were going through the honeymoon phase of our relationship, and I hadn't noticed any red flags or problems. But after a couple of months, she began to change. I noticed she had become distant, and we began arguing about minor things. I also noticed she had become somewhat cynical and negative, always complaining about things. She began making excuses to avoid having sex, and she refused to talk to me about what was bothering her. No matter how hard I tried, she wouldn't open up to me and tell me what was going on.

One day we were having a heated argument, and I told her that things really needed to change if we were going to get married. I told her I was unwilling to walk on eggshells every time she came home because I didn't know what kind of mood she would be in. I threatened to leave the relationship if she wasn't willing to deal with whatever was bothering her. I then screamed at the top of my lungs, "You have to tell me if I've done something wrong so I can fix it!"

All of a sudden, she got very quiet, and her demeanor changed dramatically. She then began to cry and said, "It's not you, it's me!" "What do you mean by that?" I asked. "I don't want to talk about it," she said. "We have to talk about it. That's the only way to fix it." "I told you, I don't want to talk about it," she said angrily. "Well, if you aren't willing to talk about it, how can we fix it? And if you're unwilling to fix it, there is no reason for us to continue this relationship."

"What are you saying? Are you saying you want to break up with me?"
"I'm saying if you're unwilling to talk about what's bothering you, there is no way we can fix it. And if we can't fix it, why should we continue being unhappy?"

Once again, she became very quiet as tears rolled down her face. She then said she had to tell me something that she had never told anyone before and made me promise to never tell anyone. Through her tears, she told me she had been raped. It had happened a very long time ago, but the experience was still having an impact on her and causing problems in our relationship.

Because of my own experience with sexual abuse, I felt a deep sense of compassion and empathy towards her. Now things began to make sense, and I began to understand why our relationship had changed. I embraced her and told her we could work through it. I told her I was willing to do whatever it took to help her move through her pain. I told her I was willing to go to therapy with her or do a workshop or seminar that could help her get through the trauma. But she refused. She said she had tried therapy, and it didn't work, and she was unwilling to try again.

After a few months, we were still miles apart. Her refusal to go to therapy and her unwillingness to heal her trauma created a massive wall between us. There was no intimacy or connection, and we were drifting further and further apart. And so I had to make a choice: should I stay with this woman whom I loved, but who was unable to accept the love I was trying to give her, or should I let her go in order to be happy?

It was an extremely difficult decision, but eventually, I decided to walk away. I had honestly done everything I could to love her and support her in dealing with her trauma, but I learned you can't help someone who isn't willing to help themselves. It was a difficult decision, but it was definitely the right decision.

I shared that story because I believe healing from trauma is possibly one of the most important topics we don't talk about often enough in the Black community. Most of us are aware of the impact of cultural trauma like slavery, police brutality, and senseless acts of violence, but we refuse to acknowledge the trauma that comes from within our own families and neighborhoods.

Another way to look at healing from trauma is to make peace with your past. I once had a very good friend of mine share a powerful truth that helped me understand the power of making peace with my own. I had done a lot of personal development programs, but I was still in denial about the trauma I had experienced as a child. Then one day, while speaking with my friend, she said something that really stood out for me. It was a statement that was so powerful it literally caused me to rethink everything I had learned in the personal development arena. She looked at me and said, "I don't care how positive you are, how many books you read, or how many seminars you go to. Until you make peace with your past, you will never truly be happy."

It was this statement that challenged me to thoroughly examine my entire philosophy on personal development.

I then realized that all the motivational seminars and books I had read did not help me make peace with my past, so I decided to make it the number one priority in my life. I intuitively knew that making peace with my past was the missing link to finding true happiness.

I ran across a quote by author and spiritual teacher Iyanla Vanzant that fully embodies why making peace with your past is so important. This powerful quote holds the key to your happiness, and I suggest that you read it slowly (and several times) and intently so that you fully grasp the implications of its message:

"Until you heal the wounds of your past, you are going to bleed. You can bandage the bleeding with food, with alcohol, with drugs, with work, with

cigarettes, with sex; but eventually, it will all ooze through and stain your life. You must find the strength to open the wounds, stick your hands inside, pull out the core of the pain that is holding you in your past—the memories—and make peace with them."

Herein lies the key to your happiness. What I've learned over the last twenty years is that we must be willing to heal our hearts and make peace with our past if we truly want to be happy. We can read all the self-help books in the world and listen to audio programs or go to seminars with motivational speakers, but if we fail to carry out our healing work, we will unconsciously sabotage our lives and ultimately keep ourselves from being completely happy.

Amazingly, some people do not believe that their childhood can actually have an adverse effect on their adult lives. Have you ever heard someone say that their parents used to beat them when they were little, yet they still turned out okay? This statement is a defense mechanism that keeps people trapped in their pain, and they will rationalize that their traumatic childhoods had no effect on them whatsoever.

The truth is, if you remember being beaten as a child and you have not done any healing work, I can assure you that it will have an effect on your life today.

If you remember the part about the subconscious mind, which I talked about in the first chapter, this should make sense to you. There are negative beliefs that you may have stored about yourself that could be causing you to unconsciously sabotage your life. This can show up as failed relationships, anxiety, depression, anger issues, or an overall feeling that something is simply missing from your life.

The key to making peace with your past lies in your willingness to heal any emotional scars that you may be carrying from your childhood.

What Iyanla Vanzant meant when she said, "You must find the strength to open the wounds, stick your hands inside, pull out the core of the pain that is holding you in your past, the memories, and make peace with them," is that it is your responsibility to look within your own heart and find where the pain is, and be willing to heal that pain.

There are some people who subscribe to the idea that you do not have to address your childhood wounds in order to be successful and happy. They believe that it does not do any good to "dig up" old hurts. I completely disagree with this way of thinking. I believe that it is absolutely imperative that you are willing to look at the dark events in your life and are willing to shed light on them. If you are unwilling to do so, those dark places will eventually sabotage your happiness.

There is a term called "spiritual bypassing," which means a person refuses to heal their inner wounds because they have accepted a specific religious teaching that says that God can heal them. I used to hold that belief. At one time, I thought that if I prayed enough and followed religious dogma and doctrine, then I would eventually become happy.

My own experience has taught me otherwise. It wasn't until I became courageous enough to make peace with my past and deal with some childhood trauma that I was able to heal my heart and become genuinely happy.

When I decided that I wanted to heal my wounds, I was introduced to a man named John Bradshaw, who facilitated a program called Healing Your Inner Child. In one of his workshops, I learned how my abusive childhood was at the core of all the dysfunction in my life. I learned that I had abandonment issues as a result of being separated from my mom when I was six years old, and I also learned that for the majority of my adult life, I was driven by a deep sense of shame.

It was my internal feelings of shame that drove me to be successful. I worked really hard to gain other people's approval because deep down, I didn't feel worthy.

Although it was extremely difficult, I made the choice to heal my heart and make peace with my past. I took Iyanla's advice and found the strength to open my wounds and stick my hands inside and pull out the core of my pain that was keeping me trapped in my past—and I made peace with them.

As a result of doing this work, I can honestly admit that in this very moment, I am happier today than I've ever been in my life. It definitely wasn't easy, but I can assure you that it was worth it.

I hope that you will take some time and really think about what I've just shared. Do not make the same mistakes that I did by thinking that just being positive will solve all of your problems. Of course, there is absolutely nothing wrong with being positive, and I am still a huge advocate of positive thinking. The key is to make sure that you aren't hiding behind positivity because of some unresolved emotional pain, the way I did.

If you are committed to making peace with your past and are looking for some ways to do so, let me share a few insights for you to consider.

The path to healing isn't linear, and it's different for everyone. What matters is taking that first step—whether it's scheduling a therapy session, joining a support group, or simply acknowledging that you deserve healing and happiness. Remember that seeking help isn't a sign of weakness; it's an act of courage and self-love that can transform not only your life but the lives of future generations.

As you embrace your healing journey, know that you're not just doing this for yourself. You're breaking cycles, creating new patterns, and opening yourself to the love and connection you deserve. Your healing is an act of revolution—a declaration that Black women deserve to be whole, healthy, and deeply loved.

The path to authentic love often begins with healing, and that healing starts with you. Take that first step. Your future self—and your future relationships—will thank you for it.

Healing is a deeply personal journey, and for many Black women, it often means navigating not just the day-to-day challenges of life, but also the hidden emotional scars left from childhood trauma and unresolved conflicts. These early wounds, when left untreated, can cast long shadows over a woman's life, shaping her relationships, self-image, and even her ability to experience love and intimacy.

Childhood trauma, whether from neglect, abuse, or abandonment, can profoundly affect how Black women relate to others, especially in intimate relationships. These early experiences often teach women, consciously or unconsciously, that the world is unsafe, people are untrustworthy, and vulnerability is dangerous. As a result, many Black women may develop emotional walls, making it difficult to let others in or truly connect on a deep level.

For example, a woman who grew up in a home where emotional support was absent may struggle to accept love and affection from a partner. She may fear rejection, abandonment, or emotional pain, leading her to self-sabotage relationships before they have a chance to flourish. This protective mechanism, while born out of survival, can keep her from experiencing the kind of deep, loving connections she truly desires. This is what happened to my former girlfriend. She sabotaged our relationship because she was unwilling to heal from her trauma.

In some cases, unresolved trauma can lead to patterns of emotional avoidance. This manifests as a reluctance to engage in emotionally intimate conversations or a tendency to shut down when a partner tries to connect on a deeper level. What often underlies these behaviors is a profound fear of being hurt again. However, the very defense mechanisms designed to protect her from pain end up keeping her isolated, disconnected, and unable to fully receive the love she deserves.

Unresolved emotional conflict from childhood trauma often leads to a search for escape, and for many Black women, this can result in addictive behaviors. Whether it's overeating, shopping, substance abuse, or work-aholism, these behaviors serve as temporary distractions from the pain. They offer fleeting relief, but they ultimately perpetuate a cycle of avoid-ance, leaving the root cause of the pain unaddressed.

Addictions, in their many forms, often act as coping mechanisms for managing the overwhelming emotions that come with trauma. Instead of facing the hurt head-on, many women may turn to these behaviors to numb their feelings of inadequacy, loneliness, or unworthiness. However, this only deepens the emotional wounds, creating more shame, guilt, and self-doubt, which in turn reinforces the cycle of addiction.

It's essential to understand that addictive behaviors are not a sign of weakness or failure. They are often symptoms of deeper, unresolved emo-tional conflicts that need healing. By acknowledging this and seeking help, Black women can begin the process of breaking free from these destructive patterns and reclaiming their lives.

The path to healing begins with recognizing the need for support. One of the most transformative steps any woman can take is seeking pro-fessional help, whether through therapy or coaching. Both therapy and coaching provide safe, nonjudgmental spaces where Black women can ex-plore their past traumas, uncover emotional wounds, and begin the heal-ing process.

Therapy, particularly trauma-informed therapy, is a powerful tool for addressing the deep emotional scars left by childhood trauma. Therapists can help women identify the root causes of their pain, process their emo-tions, and develop healthier coping mechanisms. They guide women through the stages of grief, anger, sadness, and, ultimately, acceptance, helping them release the hold that trauma has on their lives.

Coaching, on the other hand, offers a more forward-focused approach. Life coaches can help Black women set goals, create action plans, and build the confidence needed to move past their trauma and into a space of growth and transformation. While therapy delves into the past, coaching focuses on the future, empowering women to take control of their lives and make choices that align with their highest selves.

Together, therapy and coaching can provide a comprehensive approach to healing and transformation. Therapy helps Black women process their past, while coaching equips them with the tools they need to create a brighter, more fulfilling future. Both are invaluable on the journey to wholeness.

Healing also requires a deep commitment to self-love. For many Black women, the world has not always been kind or affirming. Society often places undue pressure on Black women to be strong, resilient, and self-sacrificing. While these traits are admirable, they can sometimes lead to a neglect of self-care and self-compassion.

Learning to love oneself—flaws, scars, and all—is a vital part of healing. This means embracing vulnerability, accepting imperfection, and understanding that worthiness is inherent. It also means surrounding oneself with a supportive community that nurtures healing and growth. This could be through women's groups, spiritual communities, or simply cultivating relationships with those who genuinely care about one's well-being.

The journey of healing is not just about overcoming trauma; it's about creating new narratives for oneself. Black women have the power to break free from the cycles of trauma, addiction, and emotional pain, and to redefine their stories. By investing in their healing through therapy, coaching, and self-care, they can transform their lives in profound ways.

Healing is not linear, and it often requires patience and persistence. But by committing to the process, Black women can move from a place of survival to a place of thriving. They can experience the deep, meaningful connections they crave, free from the burdens of the past. They can break the chains of addictive behaviors and step into their power as fully healed, whole individuals.

In the end, healing and transformation are not just possible—they are the birthright of every Black woman. And through this journey, she can reclaim her voice, her power, and her ability to love and be loved in the most authentic and fulfilling ways.

I'd like to close this chapter by sharing an article I wrote about my experience with therapy. My hope is that it will not only shed light on the importance of therapy, but **it** will also give you permission and the courage to seek support if needed.

Men's Emotional Healing

In 1989, I had a series of traumatic experiences that were beginning to take their toll. My divorce and separation from my kids were extremely painful and had begun to negatively impact my life. I had slipped into a deep state of depression and was barely able to function on a daily basis. As my depression deepened, I went into isolation, where I literally shut myself off from the outside world.

Although I was able to go to work and function in that capacity, I was completely disconnected from any social settings. I was not dating, and I did not socialize with my friends. I also had difficulty sleeping. I would rarely eat, and I had begun to lose weight, which was rare for me, being a former personal trainer that took excellent care of my physical body.

After several months, I began to have fleeting thoughts of suicide, and it appeared that my situation was hopeless. In an effort to alleviate some of the pain, I began to read books dealing with depression.

As I read them, I could see myself in some of the stories. I definitely had all of the symptoms of depression, and I knew that I had to deal with it head-on if I ever wanted to get my life back on track. After reading several books, I realized that I was still deeply depressed and had not really begun to deal with the issues that were causing my depression. Instinctively, I knew that I needed help, and I decided that I would seek therapy.

After making the decision to get help, another series of challenges surfaced. First of all, how was I going to find a therapist? How would I know which one to choose? What if the therapist couldn't help me? Would I be able to change? Could therapy "fix" me? What about the money to pay for it? I was completely broke and definitely couldn't pay someone to listen to my problems. What was I going to do? These were just a few of the questions that were going through my mind.

My greatest fear was wondering what would happen if my employees found out. As a manager, I was considered the leader, and I definitely didn't want to appear weak in front of my co-workers. I believed that I needed to keep this a secret so that I would not lose the respect of my employees. In addition, I did not want my superiors to know because I thought I might lose my job if they found out.

After a few months of agonizing over these questions, I knew that I had to take the chance and try therapy. I didn't have any other choice. It was to seek help or die—there was no gray area. I decided that I definitely wanted to live, and I somehow gained the courage to seek a therapist.

My first attempt at therapy did not go well. I walked into the therapist's office and pretended that I was seeking information for a friend. I'm sure the people there knew this was a lie, but they allowed me to walk out with some of their brochures and a phone number for their suicide hotline.

To be honest, I was absolutely terrified. But although I was scared, deep down I knew that I would have to gain the courage to try again. I waited a few days and tried a different therapist's office. This time I had a completely different result.

As I walked into the office, I believe the receptionist picked up on my fear. I began asking her questions about depression and whether or not they had any books that I could read. All of a sudden, a therapist walked out and began asking me questions.

"May I help you?" she asked.

"Not really, I'm just looking for a little information about depression."

"Are you depressed?" "I'm not really sure," I answered.

"Why don't you come inside and let's talk a little. Is that alright?"

"I guess so."

As I followed her into her office, it felt as if my heart was going to jump out of my chest. I was so nervous and afraid that I was literally dripping with sweat. She obviously picked up on this and began to put my mind at ease.

"What is your name?"

"Michael."

"Well, Michael, I can sense that you are a little nervous, so let me start by asking what I can do to help you. Is there anything I can do for you?"

"Well maybe. I have been doing some research about depression, and I think I'm depressed, but I'm really not sure."

"Do you feel depressed?"

"Based on what I've read so far, I think I am. But to be completely honest, I'm not sure I know exactly what depression is supposed to feel like. Does that make any sense to you?"

"It makes a lot of sense to me. Unfortunately, most men do not recognize how they feel. Men have been conditioned to disconnect from their emotions, and that makes it extremely difficult for them to express how they really feel. Most men will tell you what they think, but they usually do not know how they feel. You apparently fit into this category."

"I'm not sure if I really understand what you're saying, but a part of me thinks that you're right."

"You just validated the point I made. You are currently speaking from an intellectual perspective, instead of an emotional one. It sounds as if you are disconnected from your emotions."

"Let's assume that you're right. If I am disconnected from my emotions, how do I get reconnected? Do you have any books on how to do this?"

"Unfortunately, you cannot reconnect to your emotions by reading books. In order for you to reconnect, you have to relearn how to feel. This can be accomplished through therapy with me or any trained therapist."

"I really don't understand what you mean. But if I decide to relearn how to feel, how long will it take?"

"I really can't answer that question. It's really up to you and how committed you are to doing the work."

"What do you mean by doing the work? What kind of work is involved?"

"In the therapeutic community, we use the word 'work' because it takes a considerable amount of effort to heal yourself so that you can reconnect with your emotions. Doing the work means that you become willing to open yourself up on an emotional level. This can be quite difficult at times."

"Well, I believe I'm ready. I'm really tired of being alone, and I definitely want to experience some fun in my life again. I think I can do this, so how much will it cost?"

"I operate on a sliding scale based on your ability to pay. The most important thing is for you to make the commitment to yourself to heal, and we can address the money issue at a later date. Are you ready to begin? Let's set up a date and time for you to begin your healing."

"I just wanted to thank you for being so nice and understanding. The truth is I was about to run out of your office before you showed up. Now I am really glad that I came because I really believe that you can help me."

"That is a great attitude to have. I'm glad that you trust me enough to work with you. Just remember that I can guide you, but you must be willing to do the work. As long as you believe that you can heal, I can assure you that you will. Just stay committed and trust the process, and you will be just fine. The truth is, you have already done the hard part by showing up today. It takes an incredible amount of courage to be here, and I'm proud of you for taking the first step."

As I left the therapist's office that day, I knew I had just taken the biggest step of my life. I didn't know what to expect, but I knew I was willing to do whatever it took to heal my emotions and relearn how to feel. I became committed to my own healing, and I can now say that I'm emotionally healed and connected to my authentic self.

As the therapist mentioned, it wasn't easy, but it was definitely possible. It has been one of the most challenging, yet most fulfilling, journeys of my life.

I cannot put into words the joy I feel on a regular basis as a result of doing my emotional work. My relationships now work, my creativity and sense of reverence have enhanced, my love of nature has been rekindled, and my professional life is rewarding and fulfilling. I took the road less traveled, and it has made all the difference in the world for me.

I wanted to share this story because there is such a negative stigma about men and therapy that I believe it's time for a new conversation. In this new conversation, men will recognize the importance of healing their emotions, and they will put forth the effort to do their healing work.

When we learn to support each other in our growth, we can remove the fear and stigma of being emotionally vulnerable, which will ultimately result in us being happier human beings. I personally believe that this is the most important work men can participate in, and we must begin supporting each other through this process.

If we gain the courage to do this work, we will see a decline in domestic violence, child abuse, alcoholism, and random acts of violence. The time has come for a new conversation about our emotional healing. Are you willing to join in the conversation?

"*The ultimate measure of a man is not where he stands in moments of comfort and convenience, but where he stands at times of challenge and controversy.*"
— Martin Luther King Jr.

CHAPTER 4

Black Men Are Awesome

When we talk about Black men in the media or everyday conversations, it's easy to get caught up in negative stereotypes and misconceptions. These harmful narratives have seeped into our culture for generations, distorting the image of Black men in ways that often affect relationships between Black men and Black women. For Black women, these stereotypes can fuel mistrust and skepticism, leading to misconceptions that prevent us from seeing the beauty, strength, and love that Black men possess.

In this chapter, we will explore some of the common misconceptions Black women may have about Black men and shed light on why these perceptions should change. More importantly, we will offer reasons to embrace a new, empowering vision of Black men as loving partners, caring fathers, and leaders in creating strong Black families.

1. The "Absent Father" Myth

One of the most pervasive stereotypes about Black men is that they are irresponsible or unwilling to be involved in their children's lives. The image of the absent Black father is pushed heavily in mainstream media, overshadowing the many examples of Black men who are deeply committed to raising their children with love and dedication. In reality, studies have shown that Black fathers who live with their children are just as involved, if not more so, in their children's day-to-day lives compared to fathers of other ethnic groups.

2. The "Commitment-Phobic" Narrative

Another common misconception is that Black men are afraid of commitment or unwilling to build long-term relationships. This stereotype portrays Black men as perpetual bachelors, uninterested in marriage or forming deep, loving bonds. While it's true that relationships are complex and challenging, it is unfair and inaccurate to label all Black men as emotionally unavailable. Many Black men desire the stability and partnership that comes with marriage and are actively seeking to create strong, lasting connections.

3. The "Unemotional" or "Cold" Stereotype

Black men are often unfairly portrayed as emotionally distant or incapable of expressing love and affection. This stereotype dehumanizes them by suggesting that they lack the ability to show vulnerability or care deeply for their partners. Yet, many Black men are incredibly compassionate and deeply connected to their emotions. They are capable of love, tenderness, and empathy—they just express it in ways that may not always align with societal expectations.

4. The "Aggressive and Hyper-Masculine" Perception

Black men are frequently viewed as overly aggressive, violent, or hyper-masculine. This misconception is rooted in a long history of racial prejudice, but it still has damaging effects on relationships between Black men and women. The truth is that most Black men are gentle, thoughtful, and protective, not out of aggression but out of a genuine desire to care for and protect their loved ones.

Despite these stereotypes, Black men continue to defy these misconceptions every day. As Black women, it's important to recognize the beauty and potential in Black men, and shift your perspective to see them for who they truly are—loving, caring, and capable partners. Here are a few reasons why Black women should embrace this new view of Black men:

1. Black Men Want Strong Families

Black men understand the importance of family and are dedicated to creating a legacy of love and unity. Many Black men are actively involved in their children's lives, providing guidance, support, and love. They see their role as fathers as an essential part of their identity and take great pride in raising children who are empowered and confident. A strong Black family begins with a strong partnership, and Black men are eager to create that foundation with Black women.

2. Black Men Are Committed Partners

Black men are more than capable of committing to long-term, loving relationships. Many Black men cherish the idea of marriage and family, and they seek to build relationships that are not only emotionally fulfilling but also spiritually aligned. The idea that Black men are not interested in settling down is simply untrue. When given the opportunity to be vulnerable and open, Black men can be some of the most dedicated and loving partners.

3. Black Men Are Resilient and Compassionate

Black men have endured generations of systemic oppression, racism, and societal pressures that have attempted to diminish their humanity. Yet, despite these challenges, they continue to show resilience, strength, and compassion. Their experiences have shaped them into men who understand the importance of love, support, and community. When Black men are loved and supported, they can offer the same in return, creating powerful, uplifting relationships with their partners.

4. Black Men Are Redefining Masculinity

More and more, Black men are challenging the traditional notions of masculinity that emphasize toughness and emotional detachment. Instead, they are embracing a more balanced approach to manhood that includes emotional intelligence, vulnerability, and deep connections with their partners. Black men are proving that it is possible to be strong and sensitive, to be a protector and a nurturer. This shift in how Black men view themselves opens the door for healthier, more loving relationships.

It's important for black women to know they have the power to change the narrative about Black men. By shedding the stereotypes and misconceptions that have clouded their perceptions, they can open themselves to the truth: Black men are awesome. They are loving, caring, committed, and fully capable of creating strong, vibrant families with us.

It's time to celebrate and uplift our Black men for who they truly are. By embracing a new perspective, we not only strengthen our relationships but also help build the foundation for a thriving Black community built on love, trust, and mutual respect. Together, Black men and Black women can create extraordinary lives, families, and legacies. All we need is the willingness to see each other with fresh eyes and open hearts.

I'd now like you to do a very simple yet extremely powerful exercise. I can assure you that if you are willing to do this exercise, it can completely change your perception about black men. To do so, takes rigorous honesty on your part and although it may make you a little uncomfortable, rest assured the exercise can be very enlightening.

All you need is a pen or pencil and a stopwatch. You can use your cellphone or look at a clock with a second hand. What you're going to do is a sentence completion exercise. I am going to write a sentence and what you're going to do is complete it and write down as many answers as you can in one minute. The key is to be honest with yourself and write down the first thing that comes to mind. Don't think to hard or long about your answer. Just write down the first things that comes to mind for one minute. Don't stop until one-minute passes. Just keep writing.

Are you ready? Do you have your pen or pencil? Are you willing to do the exercise? Are you a little nervous? It's okay! The key is to simply be honest with yourself and write down the first things that come to mind.

Here is the sentence:

Black men are....

_____

_____

_____

_____

_____

_____

_____

_____

_____

_____

_____

_____

So, how did it go? Did you complete the exercise? Were you surprised by your answers? Were you completely honest with your answers?

The purpose of the exercise was to uncover your deeply held beliefs about Black men. If you've had negative experiences with Black men, then your list should have reflected that. On the other hand, if your experience with Black men has been positive, that should have been reflected in your answers.

As mentioned in a previous chapter, our subconscious beliefs are extremely powerful. Therefore, if you have negative beliefs about Black men, you can rest assured your experience with them will most likely be negative. It is imperative for you to examine your deeply held beliefs about Black men.

To provide you with some insights on male behavior, I'd like to share an excerpt from my book, *A New Conversation With Men*. During my research for the book, I uncovered what I believe are the five most destructive beliefs that cause the majority of pain and suffering in a man's life.

They are called:

The Five Illusions of Manhood

"The people who are crazy enough to think they can change the world are the ones who do."
— Steve Jobs

This quote by Steve Jobs is one of my absolute favorites. The reason I love this quote so much is that, all my life, people have called me crazy—not in a bad way, but simply in a different way. In my heart and soul, I have always felt "different," not better than or less than anyone else, simply different from everyone else. As I reflect back over my life, I recognize that I have always been that round peg trying to fit in the square hole of society. I truly believe that I can change the world. Maybe not in the way that Martin Luther King Jr., Gandhi, or Nelson Mandela changed the world, but in my own simple way, on my own simple terms, I can and I will change the world.

Although this may sound a bit grandiose, I believe that everyone actually has the ability and capacity to change the world. We all have the ability, but very few of us have the willingness. What sets us "crazy" people apart is simply our willingness to act on our abilities.

So, what about you? Are you one of the crazy people? Are you crazy enough to believe that you can change the world? Are you willing to use your abilities to assist me in creating this new paradigm of masculinity that I'm writing about? Are you ready to fully engage in a new conversation with men and become a part of our new revolution? I believe you are, so let's examine the five illusions of manhood that every man must now be made aware of. Once men wake up from these illusions, I can assure you that a shift in male consciousness will occur, and the world will be transformed for the better.

As a result of the research and study I've done over the past twenty years, I have concluded that there are five illusions that men hold onto that cause the overwhelming majority of pain and suffering in their lives. These illusions are perpetuated through our families, our cultures, and our media. In other words, these illusions are actually an integral aspect of being caught in the drift of society. In order to break free from these illusions, a man must first become aware that they even exist. So, I would like to share these five illusions with you now:

1. To be a man, you must be non-emotional and disconnected.
2. To be a man, you must use sexual conquest as a gauge for manhood.
3. To be a man, you must have status, positions, and power.
4. To be a man, you must have money and material possessions.
5. To be a man, you must win at all costs and compete against other men.

These five illusions are the foundation of all pain and misery in a man's life. If you will take a moment and really examine them, I believe you will see what I mean. To give you a better understanding of how these illusions affect your life, I will now break them down and explain each one individually.

$$\infty$$

To be a man, you must be non-emotional and disconnected.

I believe that this is the greatest illusion. All other illusions are actually built on top of this one. In our society, males are conditioned from a very young age to not feel. We are given messages that to feel and express those feelings is somehow weak, or worse, feminine. Therefore, we start accepting this illusion even as little boys. Think about the powerful messages you received as a young boy—things like, "Big boys don't cry," "Stop being a baby," and "Don't act like a sissy." These are the beginnings of the acceptance of this illusion. What actually occurs is that we begin to shut down our emotions, and the only way to cope is to express ourselves through our intellect. We stop expressing how we feel, and we begin expressing what we think. Of course, there is absolutely nothing wrong with thinking. Using our intellect is an integral and necessary aspect of our humanity, but without our emotions, we become empty, hollow automatons that miss out on the most important aspects of our lives.

This illusion is powerful because, as men, we accept that the only appropriate feelings we should express are the negative ones. It's absolutely acceptable for a man to express anger and rage in our society without being accused of being less than a man, but if a man expresses joy, sadness, or fear, then his masculinity will always be questioned. A good example of this is a television interview with Terrell Owens, who was a wide receiver for the Dallas Cowboys football team.

After the Cowboys suffered an emotional loss to the New York Giants, Terrell defended his friend and quarterback, Tony Romo. In the interview, Terrell began to cry as he shared openly about how unfair the media was being to his friend. It was obvious that he was deeply saddened by the loss, but he was also saying just how much he cared for his friend. As a result of this interview, his masculinity was immediately challenged. The media went into a frenzy about Terrell's emotional interview. Some of the sportscasters accused him of being weak and overly sensitive, while others even questioned his sexuality by implying that he might be gay.

The question I pose to you is: why is it so unacceptable in our society for a man to be emotional? Does it really make us less than men if we are comfortable expressing our feelings and wear our hearts on our sleeves? Who decided that women could be emotional but not men?

This is accepted in our society because we are trapped in the illusion that men are supposed to be non-emotional and disconnected. It is an illusion that has been passed down for generations, and the time has come for us to wake up from this illusion. When a man is trapped in this illusion, he loses his ability to truly experience life the way it was meant to be. Without his emotions, he will miss out on the most important aspects of his life. His joy, passion, creativity, intuition, connection with his spouse and children, even his faith, are all connected to his ability to feel. So, it is important that we break free from this illusion and create a new paradigm in which men are comfortable expressing their emotions openly and honestly, without fear of having their masculinity challenged.

To be a man, you must use sexual conquest as a gauge for manhood.

If you get nothing else from this book, my hope is that you get this: this is one of the most destructive illusions perpetuated throughout our society. This illusion contributes to teenage pregnancy, divorce, rape, sexually transmitted diseases, and all sorts of violence. I cannot pinpoint when this illusion began, but I would assume that it has been around since the beginning of time. It really doesn't matter when it started; the question we must ask ourselves is how we can end it.

Think back to your youth and see if you remember how prevalent this illusion was, especially during your younger days. Do you remember when you were young and the only thing you thought about was sex? As teenagers, our minds and our hormones were obsessed with the prospect of having sex. If we are really honest with ourselves, we will recognize that almost everything we did in some way led us to try to attract the opposite sex so that we could engage in the act of sex. We bought cars to try to attract girls. We played sports hoping it would attract girls. We bought clothes and kept our hair perfect in hopes of attracting girls.

We made money to impress and attract girls. So why were we so obsessed with girls? Because we wanted to have sex! We all believed that by having sex, we would validate our manhood, and our friends would cheer for us, and we would be happy and fulfilled. So if we weren't having sex, we usually lied about it just to make sure that we maintained the illusion that we were real men. If we weren't having sex and maintaining this illusion, then we usually felt inadequate and somehow inferior as young men.

Now I would like you to fast forward to the present. If you take a moment and ask yourself the same questions, you will see that most of us as men are still trapped in the same illusion. We buy cars to attract women. We play sports to attract women. We buy clothes and keep our hair perfect to attract women. We make money and spend money to attract and impress women. So why are we so obsessed with attracting women? Because we want to have sex with women!

And when we aren't having sex with women, we're usually lying about it to our friends. Can you see the insanity in this? Sexual conquest does not make you a man. It is only an illusion and a temporary fix to your unhappiness. If you are using sex as a gauge for manhood, you are trapped in a vicious cycle of addiction and denial.

To be a man, you must have titles, positions, and power.

Have you ever noticed how our society adores celebrities, sports figures, and executives? We are taught that, "He who has the gold makes the rules," which implies that the more money you have, the "better" you are as a person. The implication is that somehow men who are wealthier or who have higher societal status are somehow "superior" to other men.

This is definitely an illusion. The truth of the matter is that monetary wealth does not make you a better man. It may, in some ways, make your life easier, but it definitely does not make a man superior to other men. The sad part is that too many men accept this illusion, and they spend all of their energy trying to move up the societal ladder to validate themselves. They invest all of their time and energy in trying to gain titles and labels, while in reality, they feel empty and unfulfilled. The way that they try to compensate for this emptiness is by acting "superior" even though they really aren't.

I must admit that I was definitely caught in this illusion twenty years ago. Although I did not consider myself to be superior to any other man, I did believe that attaining the title of "Manager" would somehow validate me as a man. Although I did not recognize it at the time, my ambition and drive were actually fueled by my own insecurities about being a man. In my mind, climbing the corporate ladder and becoming success-ful was a way to prove to myself that I was competent and intelligent. Unfortunately, even after I made it to the top, I still felt the same insecu-rities. Even though I put up the façade of being in control and in charge, there was a part of me that was a frightened little boy simply trying to find his way home.

Too many men are currently caught in this illusion of manhood. You can recognize them by their big egos and their arrogance. They parade around town flashing their titles at you and trying to get the external vali-dation they so desperately need. On the outside, they may appear to have it all together, but on the inside, they are wounded little boys doing the best they can to maintain their charade.

$$\infty$$

To be a man, you must have money and material possessions.

This illusion is the reason men spend billions upon billions of dollars buy-ing "stuff." Too many of us believe that if we just buy the right house, the right car, the right watch, or the right clothes, then we will be viewed as men, and we will gain approval from our friends. This is why so many of us feel empty and discontented—because we have bought into the illusion that if we accumulate enough "stuff," we will feel fulfilled. Nothing could be further from the truth. This illusion is why so many of us try to "keep up with the Joneses."

As I think about this illusion, I'm reminded of my high school days when I purchased my first car. My first car was a 1969 Ford Mustang that I absolutely loved. But it wasn't the freedom that came from owning my own car that excited me; it was the fact that in my mind, I had now be-come a man. Of course, I was only seventeen at the time and still living at home, but in my mind, I had graduated from adolescence and moved into manhood. (This just goes to show you how this particular illusion really kicks in during our formative high school years.)

Another way that I bought into this illusion was by pretending that I had lots of money even when I didn't. I remember keeping a big wad of cash in my pocket at all times, and I would always have a twenty or fifty-dollar bill on top with lots of one-dollar bills on the bottom. Whenever I would be out with my friends, I would pull out my wad of cash and pretend that I had a lot more money than I actually did.

Since most of my friends didn't have jobs or money, I was always seen as "The Man" to My peers. This was definitely a big boost for my ego, but it caused me to fall deeper and deeper into the illusion.

These are just two examples of the things some of us as men do when we are trapped in this illusion. Sadly, there are currently lots of men out there today who are still doing the things that I did in high school. (Are you one of them?) They are the ones who have become trapped in the illusion that they must have money and material things to be a man, and I can assure you that they are paying a significant price in terms of their emotional, psychological, and spiritual well-being.

To be a man, you must win at all costs and constantly compete against other men.

This is probably the least recognized of all the illusions. Although we seldom talk openly about this, there is an unspoken male law that says we are supposed to always compete against each other. This can be witnessed on a large scale by corporate corruption. When a man's ego gets inflated, he will do anything and everything to "stay on top." All rational thinking goes out the window if a man thinks his competitor is getting ahead of him. Our business schools teach that being competitive is the foundation of success, but they do not teach about the consequences of this overly competitive, macho position that too many men fall victim to.

A perfect example of this on a small scale is an experience I had as a salesman in a hardware store. One day, I sold a customer a very expensive barbecue grill. The customer wanted to make sure that it had all of the latest technology, and he wanted it to be the "best." I worked with him for a couple of days until I finally put together the grill of his dreams. As he walked out of the store, his final comment to me was, "Thanks for helping me put together such an awesome grill. My neighbor is going to be green with envy."

A couple of days later, a gentleman showed up and asked to speak to me about purchasing a grill. He specifically asked for me because his neighbor told him that I was very helpful. He raved about how awesome his neighbor's grill was, and he said he wanted to purchase one just like it. But then he added that he wanted to make sure it had at least one feature that his neighbor's grill did not have. He didn't care what the feature was; as a matter of fact, he even mentioned that he probably wouldn't use the new feature. He simply wanted to make sure it was better than his neighbor's grill.

This is what happens when you get caught in this illusion. You will do irrational things and then rationalize them by saying you work hard for your money and deserve to have the best. Of course, there is nothing wrong with wanting the best for yourself, but when you get trapped in this illusion, you will ultimately experience emptiness.

These are the five illusions of manhood that are perpetuated throughout our society. It is absolutely imperative that you recognize these illusions and avoid being trapped by them. The intention of *A New Conversation with Men* is to assist you in breaking free from all of these illusions, so I would now like to share some concrete things you can do to break free from them.

You must be willing to become aware that the illusion exists.

This is always the most difficult and challenging step, and at the same time, it is always the first step. As soon as you become aware that you are trapped in the illusion, you have already begun waking up from it. Take some time and reflect on these illusions, and then write down the one that resonates the most with you. By writing down the illusion, it will begin to lose its grip on you. Imagine the illusion as internal darkness and your awareness as eternal light.

By shining the light onto the darkness, the darkness disappears. Your awareness is the light that will remove the darkness. Challenge yourself to become aware of the illusion you may be caught in.

You must be willing to be transformed by the renewing of your mind.

This is what I mean by having a new conversation with men. It means becoming aware of old belief systems, thought patterns, and assumptions that may no longer be working for you. By changing your internal dialogue (conversation), you lay the foundation for new ways of being a man. Think of your mind as a garden and all of your thoughts as seeds. Whatever seed (thought) you plant has to grow. If you are planting negative seeds, guess what grows? If you are planting positive seeds, what do you think will sprout up? Transforming your mind means that you make a conscious effort to recognize what types of seeds you are planting. The more conscious you become, the more likely you are to plant positive seeds.

This also means that you become conscious of all the things you are allowing to be planted in your mind. This means you should limit your exposure to all the negative seeds planted by our media. So do yourself a favor and disconnect from too much television.

You must be willing to heal and reconnect to your emotions.

This is definitely our greatest challenge as men. As I mentioned, we are conditioned not to feel, but it is our responsibility to go against societal conditioning and become courageous enough to begin our emotional healing process. Until you learn to heal and feel, there will always be something missing in your life. I will go into greater depth and detail about this in Chapter Five, titled "Transformation."

You must seek support.

You must understand that you cannot do this alone. I understand how difficult it is for men to seek support, but the fact remains that you must seek help. I don't care if you go to therapy, join a men's group, join AA, or go to a church group. It is important that you surround yourself with like-minded men who can support and challenge you to become the best man you can be. Gaining the courage to seek support is a surefire way to help you break free from any of these illusions. I highly recommend that you join our online community at www.anewconversationwithmen.com, because it is filled with resources designed to help you break free from these illusions, and it will put you in contact with other men who are on the same journey as you. They can serve as role models and mentors for you and help you recognize that you are never alone.

You must develop a spiritual connection that works for you.

This does not necessarily mean that you have to join a church or other religious organization. It means that you must come to your own understanding that there is a power greater than yourself in the universe. By connecting to this power, it will give you strength, faith, and courage to break free from the illusions and live a more rewarding and fulfilling life.

Once you develop this connection, it is your responsibility to nurture it and ensure that you stay connected to it.

So, there you have them, the five illusions of manhood:

1. To be a man, you must be non-emotional and disconnected.
2. To be a man, you must have status, positions, and power.
3. To be a man, you must have money and material possessions.
4. To be a man, you must use sexual conquest as a gauge for manhood.
5. To be a man, you must win at all costs and compete against other men.

And these are the five things you can do to wake up from the illusions:

1. You must be willing to become aware that the illusion exists.
2. You must be willing to be transformed by the renewing of your mind.
3. You must be willing to heal and reconnect to your emotions.
4. You must seek support.
5. You must develop a spiritual connection that works for you.

In order to make the world a better place, we must recognize these illusions and remove them from our collective psyches. It begins with each man waking up and choosing to break free from these illusions. In doing so, the world will be a much better place for everyone.

Are you willing to look at the man in the mirror and ask him to change his ways?

I hope this has given you some fuel for contemplation. In no way do I mean to justify negative male behavior, but you can rest assured, if a man is acting out negatively in any way, it is because he is trapped in one of these illusions. I must admit that it is extremely difficult to get men to engage in this new conversation. I have been attacked, criticized, vilified, and called a SNAG (sensitive new age guy) for more than 20 years simply because I encourage men to get in touch with their emotions. I've had Black men say that "I was trying to be white" because I suggested they try therapy.

The good news is that more men are now open to the idea of speaking about this new conversation with men. Collectively speaking, men are beginning to open up to new ways of being and relating as men. Because of the focus on mental health, men have begun to destigmatize things like going to therapy or hiring a life coach. They are asking themselves deeper questions about what it means to be a man, and they are seeking out ways to build more rewarding and fulfilling lives.

Remember the quote I shared from Steve Jobs:

"The people who are crazy enough to think they can change the world, are the ones who do."

As mentioned, I see myself as one of the crazy ones, and in my own small way, I believe I am changing the world. With that being said, I'd like to do something that some people might consider crazy. I would like to suggest that the key to healing relationships between Black men and Black women lies in our ability to forgive each other.

Forgiveness is a powerful force, a bridge between the wounds of the past and the hope for a better future. For Black men and Black women, the journey of forgiveness holds the potential to heal old scars, rebuild trust, and restore the love that is at the heart of our shared experience. I'd like to explore the deep emotional terrain of forgiveness, where Black men are ready to take responsibility for the ways they may have hurt Black women—both consciously and unconsciously—and are asking for forgiveness to open a path toward healing and reconciliation.

Before we can move forward in healing, we must first acknowledge the pain. Black men understand that, throughout history and even today, their treatment of Black women has not always been in alignment with the respect, love, and care that Black women deserve. While the root of these behaviors is often found in the wounds inflicted by systemic racism, historical oppression, and societal pressures, that does not excuse the pain that Black women have endured.

As Black men, we acknowledge that we have sometimes fallen short. Whether through emotional neglect, abandonment, infidelity, or even perpetuating harmful stereotypes, we have caused pain to the very women who have been our strongest allies. It's time for us to stand up, take responsibility, and face the discomfort of our actions so that healing can begin.

To Black women, I say this: I'm sorry. I apologize for the times we have not shown up for you when you needed us most. I apologize for the moments when we allowed our own hurt and anger to be taken out on you, the times when our silence spoke louder than our words, and the instances when we failed to give you the love, respect, and protection you deserve.

We recognize the strength and resilience it takes to carry the emotional weight that many of you have borne in silence. We understand that our actions have often contributed to your feelings of betrayal and abandonment. And for this, we ask for your forgiveness. Not simply as a way to absolve ourselves, but as a way to acknowledge your pain, honor your healing process, and show that we are committed to change.

Forgiveness cannot be asked for lightly. As Black men, we recognize that the path to true healing requires more than just an apology. It requires us to actively engage in our own emotional growth and healing. We must take responsibility for learning how to love in healthy ways, how to communicate with empathy, and how to be emotionally available to the women who share our lives.

For too long, Black men have been conditioned to suppress their emotions and carry a facade of toughness. But we are beginning to realize that healing begins with vulnerability. It begins with looking inward and understanding our own pain, our fears, and the traumas that have shaped us. Only by healing ourselves can we offer the love, respect, and support that Black women deserve.

We take responsibility for learning to be better partners, husbands, fathers, and friends. This means being present—both physically and emotionally—in our relationships. It means learning to communicate openly and honestly, without fear or defensiveness. It means taking ownership of our mistakes, apologizing when necessary, and being willing to grow together with our partners.

Black women, we ask for your forgiveness not out of expectation, but out of a genuine desire to make things right. We understand that forgiveness is a process, and it may not happen overnight. The wounds of the past run deep, and we do not take lightly the emotional labor you have already invested in our healing.

We ask for forgiveness because we recognize that the healing of Black love depends on it. When we are able to forgive one another, we create space for understanding, compassion, and growth. Forgiveness allows us to let go of resentment and anger, and to replace it with the possibility of a brighter, more loving future.

Forgiveness is not about forgetting the past; it is about acknowledging it, learning from it, and choosing to move forward together. We ask for your forgiveness so that we can begin to heal the collective wounds that have kept us apart. We ask for your forgiveness so that we can rebuild the trust that has been broken. And most importantly, we ask for your forgiveness so that we can love each other fully and without reservation.

Forgiveness opens the door to a new beginning. As Black men and Black women, we have the opportunity to heal not just our relationships, but our community as a whole. By embracing forgiveness, we can break the cycles of pain and hurt that have been passed down through generations.

Healing together means understanding that we are on the same team. Black men and Black women have always been stronger together, and our love has the power to create lasting change. When we forgive each other, we model for the next generation what it means to love deeply and unconditionally. We show our sons and daughters that Black love is powerful, resilient, and transformative.

Let us build a future where forgiveness is a foundation, where love is abundant, and where the wounds of the past no longer dictate the course of our relationships. Black men, we are committed to doing the work of healing, and we ask that you, Black women, walk with us on this journey. Together, we can create a legacy of love that will endure for generations to come.

Forgiveness is not just a gift we give to each other; it is also a form of liberation. When we forgive, we free ourselves from the chains of resentment, anger, and bitterness that have held us back for far too long. We give ourselves permission to heal, to love, and to move forward without the weight of the past burdening our hearts.

As Black men, we recognize that the healing process is ongoing, and we are committed to it. We ask for your forgiveness so that we may walk this path of healing and reconciliation together. Black love is worth fighting for, and forgiveness is the first step in that fight.

Let us embrace forgiveness as a way to heal the past and build a future where Black men and Black women stand united in love, respect, and partnership.

During a workshop with my mentor, Dr. Wayne Dyer, he shared a powerful story about forgiveness. During the story, he asked if anyone had ever heard of someone dying from a snakebite. Most people raised their hands and said they had at least heard of people dying from a snakebite. He then said, "No one has ever died from a snakebite. People do not die from the bite; they die from the poison of the snake." He then shared that anger, resentment, judgment, and hatred are like poison in our bodies. When someone hurts us, it's like the bite—it hurts temporarily, but it doesn't kill us. But when we hold on to the anger, resentment, judgment, and hatred, it is like the poison, and it is the poison that can kill us.

This is a very powerful metaphor that teaches us about the importance of forgiveness. Forgiveness isn't about the other person; it doesn't mean you condone their behavior, and it doesn't mean they didn't hurt you. It means you are willing to let go of the poison so it doesn't kill you.

There is a story of two monks who are walking through the woods when they come across a woman who is trying to walk across a stream. In their tradition, they were not supposed to talk to or touch women. One of the monks picks up the woman and carries her across the stream and then sets her down. They continue walking through the woods for a few miles when, all of a sudden, the other monk bursts out with anger. "I can't believe you broke our tradition and carried that woman across the stream." The other monk looked at him and said, "I only carried her for ten feet; you've been carrying her for a few miles."

Forgiveness is about letting go of the poison of anger, resentment, judgment, and hatred. It's about releasing the burden of past hurts and disappointments. As you think about the men who may have hurt you, ask yourself if you are willing to let go of the poison and forgive them. If the answer is yes, then find a place in your heart to let go of the poison in order for you to be free.

"Love is a force more formidable than any other. It is invisible—it cannot be seen or measured, yet it is powerful enough to transform you in a moment, and offer you more joy than any material possession could."
— Barbara De Angelis

CHAPTER 5

∞

Loving Connections

After my divorce, the first words out of my mouth were, "I am never going to get married again." (Sound familiar?) Of course, my male ego kicked in and rationalized it by saying that I was now free to play the field. The truth was, I didn't want to experience the pain of divorce again, so I was really unconsciously setting myself up to avoid that pain.

At first, I went into isolation and threw myself into my work. I didn't date for several months because I felt like I had this huge "D" stamped on my forehead. The most painful part of my divorce was the experience of failure. I had never really failed at anything in my life, and this was a major blow. Of course, there's the embarrassment and humiliation of having to tell all your friends that you failed, and that really hurt.

After several months, I decided that it was my responsibility as a man to be in a relationship. Since I have never been shy, finding a date was relatively easy, but my first relationship after my divorce was a complete disaster. The woman I was dating was very supportive. She tried to get me to open up to her, but at the time there was still too much pain. She knew that I wasn't ready to be involved in an emotional relationship, and when she tried to relay that to me, I became extremely defensive. I told her that I had laid the ground rules early, and she had agreed to adhere to them.

The ground rules were as follows:

Rule 1: I have no problem with monogamy, so I expect the same from you.

Rule 2: I love great conversation, so be ready to discuss any and everything.

Rule 3: I have a great sense of humor and love to laugh, so be prepared to giggle.

Rule 4: I love to support people, so feel free to say whatever you feel.

Rule 5: I do not want any emotional attachment. You can lean on me, but don't expect that to be reciprocated. Breaking this rule overrides all other rules and will result in the termination of this relationship.

When Rule #5 was broken, I ran like a scalded dog.

That relationship lasted approximately two months. The next relationship lasted about six months, but she broke Rule #5, and off I went into the wild blue yonder.

I was getting tired of this relationship game and had almost come to the conclusion that there wasn't such a thing as a good relationship. As far as I was concerned, it was a societally forced phenomenon designed to cause massive amounts of pain. So I chose not to participate for a while. After a few months, I gathered some new insight and decided to give relationships one more try.

A very good friend of mine set me up on a blind date. I really trusted her judgment, so I figured I really didn't have much to lose. My date and I met at a restaurant. I was very impressed by her physical appearance. She was extremely attractive, and after our conversation began, I realized she was intelligent and confident as well. After a three-hour conversation, we decided to see each other again. As I left the restaurant, I was glad I hadn't given up on relationships. A part of me knew that she was a very special lady. We started spending a lot of time together, and for the first time in what seemed like years, I had something to be happy about. She was wonderful.

With her, I could be myself, and we spent a lot of time just being silly. Our situations were very similar, and we had a lot in common. Then

I started to remember how my other relationships had turned out, and I knew I needed to lay down my ground rules. To my surprise, she had no objections to any of them. As a matter of fact, she had the same rules herself.

Boy, was I happy! This was the perfect relationship in my opinion. I didn't have to risk being hurt emotionally, and I had the freedom to do as I pleased. It just didn't get any better than that. Things were going extremely well. Although we agreed that we could see other people, we spent most of our free time together. Of course, when you spend quality time with someone the way we did, there is no way you can avoid developing some emotional attachment. And that is exactly what started to happen.

I truly loved being with her. As a matter of fact, I began to fall in love with her. Of course, I couldn't tell her that because I had set the ground rules, and I knew they worked both ways. I surely didn't want to risk losing her, so I kept my feelings to myself. Then one night, while we were together, she embraced me and said, "I love you, Michael."

Although I felt the same way, I reacted totally differently.

"Why did you have to say that?" I asked.

"Because I mean it, that's why," she responded.

"But you know the ground rules. We both agreed that there would be no emotional bonds between us."

"I don't care about the damn ground rules. I've been trying to keep how I feel about you inside, but I can't do it any longer. If that's a problem for you, then I'm sorry. But I can no longer hide how I feel about you. We've spent the last year pretending to be just friends, but you and I both know that it's a lot deeper than that. Do you think that I'm just having sex with you? Well, I'm not; I'm making love to you, and they're not the same. So, be totally honest, how do you feel about me?"

"Well, I didn't mean for it to happen this way, but I love you too. It's been a long time since I've been happy, and you have been the source of that happiness. I've been wanting to say 'I love you,' but I was afraid that it would scare you away. I'm really glad that you shared how you feel about me because now I can do the same."

That's what my heart wanted to say, but because of my past failed relationships and my fear of getting emotionally close, this is what came out:

"I really like you a lot, but I'm not ready for any type of commitment. I realize we have fun together, but I've got a lot of things to deal with right now. The last thing I need to deal with is the complexities of a committed relationship. Remember, we both agreed on that at the beginning."

"I don't give a damn about what we agreed on at the beginning. I'm talking about right now. How do you feel right now? I'm not asking for a committed relationship; I'm not asking to take up any more of your time; I'm not going to make your life any more complex than it is right now. I simply want to know how you feel at this very moment. Would you please give me an honest answer?"

"I don't know. I really don't want to talk about this right now. Why did you have to bring this up in the first place? Everything was perfect. Now you've ruined everything."

"I haven't ruined or changed anything. I'm asking you a very simple question. Do you love me?"

"I honestly don't know. I enjoy your company, and I look forward to the times that we're together. But I honestly don't know if I love you or not."

There was silence, and I knew I had just lost the woman that I really loved. As I lay beside her, my heart really wanted to tell her, but the words would not come out of my mouth. I felt a deep sadness, and I knew it was the last time we would be together. I tried to hold her, but she was as cold as ice. I knew I had no one to blame but myself.

Initially, my ego kicked in, and I convinced myself there were plenty of fish in the sea and it was her loss in leaving me. But deep down inside, my heart was really broken.

At the time, I had no idea why I couldn't tell her how I felt. But after really addressing my emotional issues, I've come to realize that the reason I couldn't tell her how I felt was because of my fear of intimacy. I was afraid that if I told her how I felt, she would ultimately do as all the other women had done in my life: leave!

The sad part about that was she didn't want to leave. She honestly loved me and wanted nothing more than to share her love with me. I was the one who pushed her away.

There is a saying that goes: "If one person calls you a jackass, don't worry about it, but if two or more do, then you had better get a saddle." I knew that it was time for me to get a saddle. As I looked at my past failed relationships, there was one common denominator—me. And I committed myself to deal with my own "stuff" so I could create the type of relationships I knew I deserved.

Take a moment and ask yourself if you see the same pattern in your relationships. I wanted to share that story because we must understand that all relationships start with us. In the beginning, I was blaming the women I was dating for being the problem, but the truth was, I was the one who needed to address my own fears. It takes an incredible amount of honesty to take responsibility for creating great relationships. But as I've mentioned, the first relationship we must develop is the one with ourselves. So I would like to make some suggestions for creating great relationships.

As mentioned in a previous chapter, to do this, I had to be willing to make peace with my past. I had to be willing to heal my heart from past hurts and the trauma of my childhood. I had to remove my fear of abandonment and learn to trust that I was lovable and deserving of love, and accept that women could be trusted with my heart, but I had to be willing to remove the wall I had built around it to let their love in.

Therefore, I decided to take M. Scott Peck's advice and take the road less traveled. I committed to learning how to become emotionally available and refrained from relationships for five years while I healed my heart and focused on learning how to love myself. It was a challenging journey, but in the end, it paid off with huge dividends, and as a result, I was able to find the woman of my dreams to whom I've been blissfully married for the past 23 years.

Unlike teenage love, mature love is a lot deeper and more gratifying. It's about accepting the other person for who they are, not how they look or what they have. It's about loving them for their soul and loving the essence of who they are. It is a spiritual connection of the soul in which two people create a spiritual bond that cannot be broken because it is based on what's on the inside of the person, not on anything external.

So, what is the key to creating great relationships and having deep connections with others? Creating a great relationship with yourself. This means you are willing to identify any unhealed traumas from your childhood or adulthood. The adage is true: "You can never truly love another until you learn to love yourself." So, self-love is the key to creating great relationships.

Now, I would like you to take a moment and ask yourself if you see any patterns in your relationships. Remember what the quote said about being the jackass? This takes rigorous honesty on your part and can be difficult to accept, but you must understand that the only way out is through you. You must be willing to go through the things that keep you from connecting with others. So, you must identify the patterns and commit to breaking them. You may need some support to do so, so do not be afraid to reach out to a therapist or a coach to support you.

Once you've done your inner work and are ready to find your perfect partner, here are a few things you can do to help you create a lifelong love affair.

A guy named David Hawkins wrote an amazing book called *Power Versus Force*. In the book, he created something called a Map of Consciousness Scale.

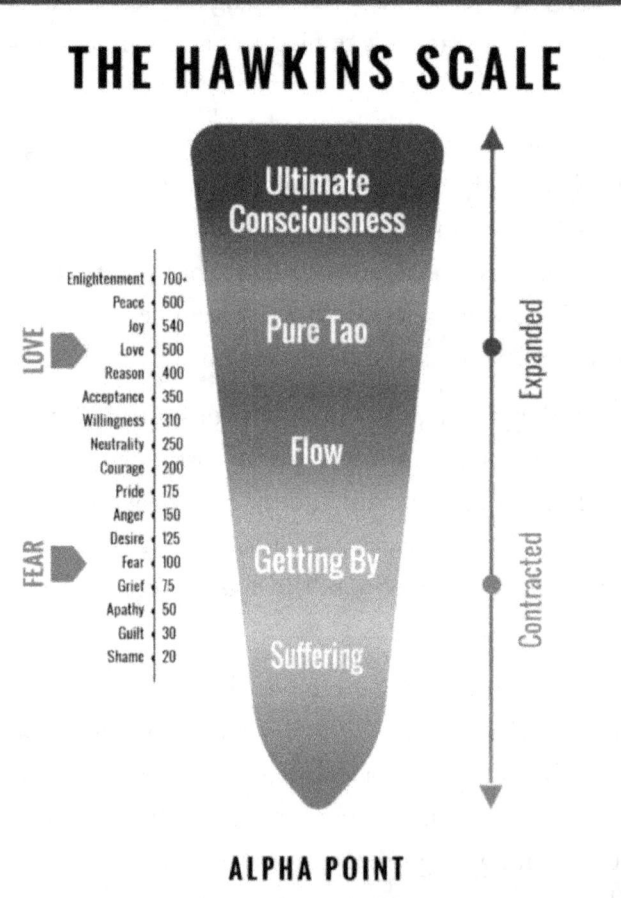

The scale starts at the bottom at 20 and moves up to 700–1000. Think of the numbers as vibrational levels. All human beings are energetic beings that vibrate at different levels, and this scale will explain what those levels are. It's important not to judge the levels as good or bad; simply see them as levels of vibration that you have complete control over.

According to David, most human beings vibrate at around 200. The point I want to make here is that it is possible to climb the ladder of consciousness to actually reach the 700 level or above if you choose to. To do this, you must be willing to get in touch with how you feel and recognize which level you are currently on.

When I was emotionally unavailable, I was probably vibrating around 20–50. I was so filled with shame from my traumatic childhood that I had very little confidence in my ability to be loved. As I did my inner work and climbed up the ladder, I became happy and secure in all areas of my life. If I had to rate myself today, based on more than 25 years of healing and transformation, I'm easily between 600 and 700. My life is filled with inner peace, joy, and purpose, and if I can get there, so can you.

To create great relationships, you must begin by recognizing where you are on this scale and be willing to climb up the scale to increase your vibration. This is why you must be willing to do your inner work and make peace with your past. If you're holding on to past hurts and negative energy, it will dictate your level of vibration, and your level of vibration will dictate what you attract into your life.

If you want to attract someone who is vibrating at a high level, you have to be vibrating at that same level. If you're vibrating at 100, you can rest assured you will only attract people who are vibrating at that level or lower. The key to creating great relationships is, first and foremost, having a great relationship with yourself. In other words, it's important to have self-love first before you can attract love into your life. Pure self-love vibrates at around 500, so your goal should definitely be to reach that level to attract that same level into your life.

If you're already in a relationship and want to deepen it, the key is to increase your vibration, and your relationship will improve. It all boils down to how you feel. Being in touch with how you feel and being willing to express how you feel is a surefire way to gauge where you are on this scale and know how well your relationship is doing.

Once you know where you are and are comfortable with your level of vibration, it's important to understand what you are looking for in a relationship if that is what you're seeking. So, let's imagine you're single and decide you want to get into a relationship. Where do you start? Obviously, the first thing you have to do is find someone to be in a relationship with, right? Let me share a brief metaphor with you to provide some insights into choosing the right person.

I want you to imagine a beautifully wrapped Christmas present. As you look at this present, you are filled with excitement and delight because the present is extremely beautiful. The present is so beautiful you want to show it off to your friends, so you take your present to a party to show it off. Once you get to the party, all of your friends begin telling you just how beautiful your present is, and you are bursting with pride.

After the party, you take your present home and can't take your eyes off it. You can't even sleep because you can't get the present off your mind. The next day, you decide to take your present to work with you. When you get to work, your co-workers are all mesmerized by the beauty of your present. Once again, you are bursting with pride as you show off your beautiful present to everyone.

One of your closest friends happens to be one of your co-workers, and they come into your office and begin asking you some questions. "Where did you find such a beautiful present? How long have you had it? What's inside of it?" Now you're beginning to get a little irritated because your friend is asking too many questions.

You then tell your friend they should be happy that you're happy to have such a beautiful present, but your friend insists that you tell them what's inside the present. Your friend grabs the present and shakes it just a bit. You become furious! "How dare you shake my beautiful present?" you say. You then tell them they do not have the right to question you about your present, and even though the present sounded like something was broken inside, you refuse to acknowledge that and chase your co-worker out of your office.

After work, you take your present home and set it on the table. You are still mesmerized by the beauty of the present, but you can't stop thinking about the sound you heard when your friend shook the package. A part of you wants to know what's inside, but another part is in complete denial and convinces you not to open it.

This goes on for a couple of weeks, and the package has begun to lose its beauty. The wrapping paper is a little torn, the ribbon has fallen off, and you aren't paying as much attention to the present anymore. You no longer take it with you, and you've lost the feeling of love and joy that you had for your present. You then decide that it's time to look inside, and when you do, you find out that it is completely broken and it's something you didn't want anyway. So, you take your present out to the dumpster and throw it in, and the next day, you start looking for a brand-new present.

This metaphor serves as a reminder of the importance of being willing to look past a person's exterior and look at the interior. Of course, it's important to find someone to whom you are physically attracted, but if that is your primary focus, you're looking in the wrong place. When seeking out a new partner, the key is to connect with who they are on the inside instead of how they look on the outside.

Just like the story, too many of us are more concerned with how our partners might look instead of who they are on the inside. This is the reason the Map of Consciousness Scale is so important. If you are willing to look inside a person and find their emotional level, you are much more likely to be compatible if their level matches yours. This was a lesson I learned due to some deep self-introspection and being willing to raise my level of vibration.

The biggest lesson I learned from my divorce was that I had absolutely no idea about the interior qualities and values I was looking for in a woman. The first time I got married, I focused on the package and not what was inside it. So, what exactly should we be looking for inside the package? I believe there are two things we must be looking for if we truly want to build a relationship that works:

1. Shared values
2. Identifying our needs

When I got married the first time, I was 21 years old, and I definitely didn't know what I was looking for. In addition to the emotional baggage I was carrying around, I was absolutely clueless about the values I had and my needs. I have come to believe that shared values are the keys to creating lasting relationships. When two people share the same values around money, sex, religion, children, and ambition, they share a great foundation on which to build a strong partnership.

So, the questions you must ask yourself are: What are my thoughts, feelings, and beliefs about money? What are my thoughts, feelings, and beliefs about sex? What are my thoughts, feelings, and beliefs about religion? What are my thoughts, feelings, and beliefs about children? What are my thoughts, feelings, and beliefs about ambition?

Take some time to think about these questions, and then put your answers on paper. Writing down your answers will give you some clarity on your values. Once you are clear on your values, whenever you choose to date someone, have an honest conversation with them about their values and see if they match yours. If they don't, it might be a good idea to look for another package. Of course, this is going to take rigorous honesty on your part. You have to be completely honest and truthful about what you value most and make sure you do not compromise your values.

This is how you begin looking inside the package. This is how you begin to learn the essence of who they are. This is where true connection happens. The second thing you must understand about yourself is your needs. As human beings, we have a lot of different needs, but in terms of relationships, we have four primary ones.

According to relationship expert Jayson Gaddis, the four primary needs all human beings have are the 4 S's: Safety, Seen, Supported, and Soothed.

Safety:

Safety is about being in an environment in which you feel safe to express yourself openly and honestly. It means being comfortable to share all aspects of yourself with your partner without fear of criticism or attack. It also means there is never any threat of physical or emotional violence, and you can simply be who you are with that person.

Seen:

Being seen means we are acknowledged for who we are, and the person we are with is able to see and appreciate who we are. It also means our experiences are validated, and even if we disagree, our point of view is allowed without attack or judgment. Being seen also means being recognized for the unique human being we are.

Supported:

Being supported means our partners are in our corners no matter what. It means they support us in pursuing our own individual interests, and they give us the space to grow. Being supportive also means standing up and speaking out to us when our partners may disagree with us and want us to see things from a different point of view.

Soothed

We all want to feel loved and accepted, and being soothed is the feeling we have when unconditional love is present. Being soothed occurs when we feel safe, seen, and supported by our partners. When these four needs are consistently met, love will blossom. Of course, this is probably easier said than done, but rest assured it is possible for you. How do I know this? Because I experience it regularly, and if I can do it, so can you.

I'd like to close this chapter with 10 Keys to Creating Healthy Relationships. Be sure to read them carefully and apply them to your life.

Number 1:

Develop a healthy relationship with yourself. For most people, I can assure you, it is very uncomfortable for them to say, "I love myself." Why? Because for some people, that may sound a little arrogant, a little cocky, a little narcissistic. The truth is, if you don't love yourself, you cannot love another person. It's not possible because all relationships begin with you.

The first thing you have to be willing to do is create a healthy relationship with yourself. When you look in the mirror, ask yourself what you see. Do you see someone who's trustworthy? Do you see someone who's lovable? Do you see someone who's dependable? Do you see someone in that mirror you want to be in a relationship with?

Ask yourself that question honestly because that's where relationships begin. They begin with you. If you want to create healthy relationships, start with yourself. Sometimes that means we have to take a break from relationships with other people and spend some time developing a relationship with ourselves. This may be uncomfortable or seem a little weird, but rest assured, it is the first thing you must do. Too many times, we want to point our fingers at the people in our lives, but the fact remains that if we want to create healthy relationships, it always begins with the person in the mirror. We must take complete responsibility for our relationships and not blame anyone else. Once we do this, we lay the foundation for great relationships.

Number 2:

Make relationships the top priority. In our culture and society, a man's job has basically been two things: protect and provide. This has been true since the beginning of time. Think about it. What was a caveman's primary responsibility? He was supposed to find a cave to keep his little cavewoman happy and warm, and then he had to go out there to find food and make sure he kept the dinosaurs from eating his family. Provide and protect.

Unfortunately, too many men are still trying to do that. They believe that if they just do these two things, they will be happy. What we really need to do if we're going to make relationships our top priority is to connect; not just provide and protect, but connect. Connection takes emotions, and men often do not have the emotional awareness to connect, which is a major cause of relationship failure.

We usually focus all of our attention on our jobs, our bills, our cars, our stuff, and our kids, but we aren't doing anything to connect in our relationships. We aren't doing anything to deepen our connection. The sad part is that many men will go through life and work at a career, raise their kids, and do everything they can to keep up with the Joneses. Then they get close to retirement and start asking themselves, "What am I going to do next?"

As soon as they retire and they're at home with their wives on a full-time basis, it's total chaos because now they have to connect with their spouse, but they don't know how to do that. If they had only made relationships the top priority in their lives from the beginning, it would have made their lives a lot easier in the long run. Be sure to make relationships the top priority in your life, and you too will be happier in the long run.

Number 3:

Relinquish the need to be right. That's it! Let go of the need to be right! It's sad, but most people would rather be right than happy. They get attached to being right, which creates disconnection, and then they wonder why they're so unhappy. Did you know that two people never have to fight in healthy, connected relationships? "What do you mean, Michael? A relationship without fighting? That's not possible!" Yes, it is! I can promise you that it is possible, and here's how: you must distinguish between fighting and conflict. They aren't the same thing.

Fighting is about being right. It's about being more concerned with being right than being happy. On the other hand, conflict occurs when you bring two human beings together who will always have different opinions and beliefs. There's no way you can avoid conflict in a relationship, but you can let go of your need to be right about the conflict, which will instantly transform your relationships.

How often have you fought over something really simple and all you had to do was say, "That's okay," and let it go? But then a part of you took this firm stand that you were just not going to let her be right. We've all done it. It's part of human nature to want to be right. Guess what? It doesn't work in relationships. Relinquishing your need to be right will transform your relationships instantly if you will just be willing to let things go. At the same time, there will be some things that you feel very strongly about, and you will choose not to compromise. You can do that without being attached to being right. You don't have to compromise your values on what's really important to you; you just have to be willing to say, "I don't have to be right. I'd rather be happy than right." When you do that, your relationships will transform immediately.

Number 4:

Be attentive to your partner. Being attentive to your partner means being in the present moment, fully aware of what they're saying, doing, and feeling. When we do that, we create a connection. When you pay attention to your partner and are really concerned about what they're saying, connection is created. If you really want to create healthy relationships, you must be attentive to your partner; again, it creates connection.

Number 5:

Express affection to your partner. That doesn't mean you have to go out in the street and kiss your wife in front of many people. Affection means that you're in some way affirming that you care about them by touching and acknowledging, and possibly kissing them. Affection doesn't necessarily mean kissing; you can just touch someone and show affection. The key is to be comfortable making physical contact with your partner. Touching is a way to create a physical connection.

Studies have shown that infants that are held, nurtured, and physically touched are healthier than babies that aren't. It's in our DNA to be touched and held. Expressing affection shouldn't be a big issue unless you're stuck in your ego, so let that go. Express affection to your partner.

Number 6:

Say, "I love you," and mean it. If you truly love someone, why should it be difficult to tell them? When you say, "I love you," be sure to say it from your heart, not your head. Say it often, and mean it every time. If you don't feel it, don't say it.

Number 7:

Spend quality time with your partner. You have to define quality time, but quality time means you move away from all the hustle and bustle of life, the kids, the jobs, the house, and all of that, and you spend time where you're just hanging out. For some, it may mean just sitting on the back porch. For others, it may be going to a spa all day. You have to decide what it is, but it's important that you spend quality time being attentive and connecting with your partner. It's extremely important.

Number 8:

Loosen up, let go, have some fun. When was the last time you laughed with your partner? Just had a good laugh? If nothing comes to mind, something's wrong because relationships should be about fun, not just about stress and all the day-to-day challenges that we deal with. If you want to create connection, you have to have fun because, whether we realize it or not, we all have this playfulness inside of us. It's there. Too many of us have pushed it down so far we've forgotten what it feels like, but we have to bring that playfulness back up and have fun and recognize that it doesn't make you less of a person to do so.

Number 9:

Celebrate your victories together. Life is tough enough as it is. Just look around you. We have all these things going on in the world. Our one refuge should be our relationship and our homes. When you accomplish something or something positive happens in your relationship, you should celebrate that. It can be something as small as a hug or something as elaborate as taking your partner out to an excellent dinner because you got a promotion at work. The key is to recognize that you're in this together, and you should be grateful that you have each other. When you overcome hurdles, it deepens your connection. Have some fun, celebrate your victories together, and acknowledge each other for being there for one another.

Number 10:

Count your blessings, not your problems. Too many times, we focus all of our attention on what's wrong versus what's right with our relationships. When you focus all of your attention on what's wrong, guess what happens... disconnection. If you're in a relationship, it may not be perfect, but you know this person is there for you, and that's something to be grateful for.

Count your blessings for what they do right. An attitude of gratitude goes a long way in deepening your connection in relationships. Make sure you're counting your blessings, not your problems. I can assure you that connection happens and relationships bloom when you do that. That's just the way it works.

There they are, the 10 Keys to Creating Healthy Relationships. I realize some of you are saying, "Okay, Michael, you've just shared ten keys to creating healthy relationships. I got it, but what I didn't get, what I didn't see, what I didn't hear you say, Michael, is anything about the sex. What about the sex, Michael? You didn't talk about the sex." Here's a promise that I can make. It's actually a guarantee. I can absolutely, 100% guarantee that if you follow these 10 keys, if you create the connection I'm talking about in relationships, there is absolutely no way you won't have great sex. Here's why: too many times, we think that sex is about the physical act; in reality, making love is about the emotional and spiritual act. When you have your emotions involved, and have a deep connection with your mate, making love is deeper, more intimate, and more awesome.

Because when you really care about somebody, it's no longer just about physical sex. It's about sharing something, sharing a part of you. This whole connection process is about moving past just having sex and making love. It doesn't mean you can't have some wild, crazy, passionate, physical love or sex. That could happen too. What I'm saying here is that we put so much focus on the physical aspect of sex that we miss out on the emotional and spiritual connection. When you do that, you cannot have great sex. If you have trust, commitment, honesty, openness, all those things in your relationships, your sex life, your love life, will work. I can guarantee you that. The question is, are you willing to accept it?

You're probably asking this, "Do these keys really work?" I know they do. How do I know? Because they work for me. If they work for me, they can work for you. More importantly, I can honestly say that I have this type of connection with my wife. I have a marriage that works because I took the time to learn about myself, I took the time to go through my emotional transformational process, and now it has allowed me to create this type of relationship.

If I can do it, you can do it too.

Before I close this chapter, I wanted to talk about interracial dating. According to most data, black women are the most faithful and dedicated women in America. My experience definitely supports that data because all of the black women I have dated were each faithful, supportive, and loyal. They are the least likely to date outside of their race and the term "ride or die" is definitely applicable to most black women.

With that being said, should black women choose to date outside of their race?

My answer is pretty simple. I've mentioned throughout this chapter the importance of creating a great relationship with yourself, and then choosing someone who shares the same values as you do. I mentioned the importance of focusing on what's inside of a person versus what's on the outside. If you do that, what difference does the color of their skin make?

I've been fortunate to have dated women from several different races and I have come to know that love and emotional connection have nothing to do with skin color. When two people are willing to really get to know each other, and are open and honest about their values around sex, children, religion, money, and ambition, they can create a connection that definitely transcends ethnicity, and they can create a lifelong love affair that is filled with trust, intimacy, love, and connection.

Isn't that what we all long for?

Embrace Connection!

Good luck!

"There is unbelievable power in ownership, and women should own their sexuality. There is a double standard when it comes to sexuality that still persists.

Men are free and women are not. That is crazy. The old lessons of submissiveness and fragility made us victims. Women are so much more than that. You can be a businesswoman, a mother, an artist and a feminist - Whatever you want to be — and still be a sexual being.

It's not mutually exclusive."
— Beyonce

CHAPTER 6

∞

Sexuality

When it comes to sexuality, Black women have often been burdened by societal and religious expectations that restrict their ability to fully embrace and express their sexual selves. Historically, Black women have been subject to harmful stereotypes that either hypersexualize or desexualize them, creating confusion and internal conflict about what it means to be both feminine and sexual. These outdated narratives have contributed to a disconnect for many Black women, preventing them from exploring their own desires, needs, and the full potential of intimacy.

It's time for Black women to reclaim their sexuality—on their own terms. This chapter explores the importance of rejecting limiting beliefs and understanding the power of sexual freedom, rooted in both self-awareness and emotional connection.

For centuries, societal expectations have dictated how Black women should view and express their sexuality. Religious beliefs, while often a source of comfort and guidance, can sometimes perpetuate the idea that sexuality is shameful or that women should be submissive in the realm of intimacy. These messages can cause Black women to suppress their natural desires, leaving them disconnected from their own bodies and their partners.

To truly experience fulfilling intimacy, Black women must begin by questioning these traditional narratives. While there's nothing wrong with choosing to follow religious values, it's equally important to recognize that expressing one's sexuality in a healthy, consensual, and emotionally connected way is a natural and empowering experience. The notion that women should be passive participants in their own sexuality, existing merely to please men, is not only outdated but harmful. Black women have the right to fully enjoy their sexual selves, and that begins with recognizing that their needs, desires, and pleasure are just as important as those of their partners.

To step into their power, Black women must embrace their femininity—both in and outside of the bedroom. Being in touch with one's femininity is about more than outward appearance or behavior; it's about feeling confident, comfortable, and in control of your body and emotions. This involves understanding and accepting your desires, being able to communicate them with your partner, and feeling empowered to take ownership of your sexual experiences.

Many Black women have been taught to see their sexuality through a lens of shame or restraint, but real intimacy and connection can only occur when there's freedom of expression. Sexuality is a vital part of who we are as humans, and it's essential that Black women give themselves permission to be free and uninhibited in their sexual lives. They should be able to express their desires without guilt, knowing that their sexuality is a part of their identity that deserves to be celebrated.

One of the key differences between simply having sex and making love is the level of emotional intimacy present in the relationship. For Black women, it's important to understand the significance of emotional connection in their sexual relationships. Intimacy isn't just about physical closeness; it's about emotional vulnerability, trust, and mutual respect. When Black women feel emotionally connected to their partners, it creates a deeper bond that elevates the sexual experience into something more meaningful.

True intimacy requires communication, openness, and a willingness to be vulnerable with your partner. This can be challenging, especially if past experiences have taught Black women to guard their hearts or suppress their feelings. But by allowing themselves to connect on an emotional level, Black women can create space for authentic and fulfilling relationships—ones that honor both their emotional and sexual needs.

It's crucial that Black women reclaim their sexual freedom and no longer see themselves solely as objects of male pleasure. Black women should understand that their sexual needs are just as important, and their desires are not something to be hidden or repressed. A healthy, balanced sexual relationship is one in which both partners feel valued, respected, and fulfilled.

Being free and uninhibited means breaking away from societal pressures and cultural norms that limit Black women's ability to express their sexuality. It's about understanding that sex is not a transaction, nor is it something to be feared. Instead, it's an opportunity to share intimacy, joy, and connection with a partner in a way that uplifts and empowers both people involved.

For Black women, reclaiming their sexuality is an essential step toward self-empowerment and fulfillment. By rejecting the constraints of societal and religious norms, embracing their femininity, and prioritizing emotional intimacy, Black women can create sexual experiences that are not only pleasurable but also deeply fulfilling.

Sexual freedom is about more than physical pleasure; it's about honoring yourself, your desires, and your right to express love and intimacy in a way that feels authentic. When Black women are free to be their true selves—unashamed, confident, and connected—they open the door to deeper love, stronger relationships, and a more empowered sense of self.

Many Black women have internalized messages that suggest they should be conservative in expressing their sexuality, or that their role is primarily to satisfy their partner's desires. These beliefs can create barriers to experiencing genuine sexual fulfillment and building authentic relationships.

It's time to challenge these limiting beliefs. Your sexuality isn't just about pleasing someone else—it's about mutual pleasure, connection, and celebration of intimacy. You have the right to express your desires, to seek fulfillment, and to expect your partner to be equally invested in your pleasure and satisfaction.

Today, it's crucial to recognize that your sexuality is a natural, beautiful part of who you are. It's not something to be hidden away or being ashamed of, but rather a vital aspect of a woman's femininity that deserves to be explored, understood, and celebrated. This doesn't mean abandoning your values or spiritual beliefs—instead, it's about finding harmony between your faith, your values, and your natural desires.

Being in touch with your sexuality starts with knowing your own body. Many of us have been taught to disconnect from our physical selves, to ignore our desires, or to focus solely on our partners' pleasure. This disconnection can lead to unfulfilling sexual experiences and shallow relationships.

Take time to understand what brings you pleasure. This isn't just about physical sensation—it's about understanding your emotional needs, your boundaries, and your desires. What makes you feel beautiful? What makes you feel powerful? What makes you feel connected? These questions are essential parts of your sexual journey.

True intimacy goes far beyond the physical act of sex. It's about creating emotional connections that make physical intimacy more meaningful and fulfilling. When we focus only on the physical aspects of sex, we miss the opportunity for deeper connection—the kind that makes love-making transcendent rather than merely satisfying.

This emotional connection requires vulnerability. It means being honest about your needs, your fantasies, and your boundaries. It means communicating openly with your partner about what you want and need, not just physically but emotionally. This level of openness can be challenging, especially if you've been conditioned to keep these thoughts to yourself, but it's essential for building truly intimate relationships.

The journey to sexual empowerment is personal and unique for each woman. There's no single "right" way to express your sexuality or experience intimacy. What matters is that you feel comfortable, confident, and in control of your sexual expression.

Remember, your sexuality is a gift to be celebrated, not a burden to be managed. When you embrace this part of yourself fully, you open the door to deeper connections, more fulfilling relationships, and a more authentic expression of who you are as a Black woman.

Now I would like to ask you a few questions. Be sure to answer them openly and honestly with yourself. You obviously do not have to share your answers with anyone, but it's extremely important for you to be honest with yourself as you answer them.

Here they are:

- Are you truly comfortable with your sexuality?
- Do you put your partner's sexual needs ahead of your own?
- Do you fake orgasms to please your partner?
- Do you hold back, allowing yourself to let go during orgasm out of fear you'll lose control and your partner will take advantage of you?
- Are you comfortable asking your partner for what you need sexually?
- Are you comfortable initiating sex?
- Are you comfortable being naked, especially with a partner?
- Do you believe sex outside of marriage is a sin?

Your answers to these questions should tell you whether or not you are truly comfortable with your sexuality. If any of these questions made you uncomfortable, it's possibly time for you to begin some sexual exploration.

I definitely don't claim to be a sex expert, but here's a list of **10 Things Black Women Can Do to Become Comfortable Expressing Their Sexuality and Femininity**:

1. Embrace Self-Love and Body Positivity
   Celebrate your body by practicing self-acceptance. Focus on the things you love about yourself, affirm your beauty daily, and challenge any negative stereotypes about Black women's bodies.

2. Educate Yourself About Sexuality
   Read books, listen to podcasts, and follow educators who focus on sexual health and femininity, especially those who celebrate the unique experiences of Black women. Knowledge helps break down barriers of shame or misinformation.

3. Explore Personal Style
   Use fashion as an expression of your femininity. Whether it's bold colors, elegant dresses, or more subtle looks, find clothing that makes you feel powerful, beautiful, and confident.

4. Surround Yourself with Positive Influences
   Engage with communities of women who celebrate femininity and embrace their sexual empowerment. Positive role models and supportive friends can help you feel more confident in your own expression.

5. Practice Self-Care Rituals
   Engage in self-care activities like spa days, meditation, or yoga. Pampering yourself reinforces your connection with your body and helps you feel more in tune with your femininity.

6. Heal Past Trauma
   Seek therapy or counseling if you've experienced trauma or negative experiences related to your sexuality. Healing emotional wounds can open the door to fully embracing your sensuality without guilt or fear.

7. Express Your Desires Openly
   Practice open communication in your relationships. Feel empowered to express your needs and desires without fear of judgment, whether in romantic, sexual, or everyday interactions.

8. Challenge Cultural Norms and Stereotypes
   Black women have often been unfairly sexualized or criticized for their femininity. Work on separating yourself from these stereotypes by acknowledging that your expression of sexuality is yours to define.

9. Engage in Feminine Arts and Hobbies
   Participate in activities like dance, painting, or poetry that celebrate feminine energy and sensuality. Expressing creativity in these ways can help deepen your connection to your feminine essence.

10. Affirm Your Sexuality as Natural and Beautiful
    Regularly affirm to yourself that your sexuality is a natural and beautiful part of who you are. Reject societal stigmas that might try to limit or shame your self-expression.

These steps can help cultivate a healthy, empowered relationship with your sexuality and femininity.

Emotional intimacy is the foundation of any healthy sexual relationship. It allows for a deeper connection beyond just the physical, creating a space where both partners feel seen, heard, and valued. For Black women, emotional intimacy plays a critical role in fostering healthy sexual relationships because it allows you to fully embrace vulnerability and trust, which are key to sexual fulfillment and satisfaction.

Here's how emotional intimacy impacts sexual relationships:

1. Enhances Trust and Vulnerability
   When you feel emotionally close to your partner, you're more likely to open up about your desires, boundaries, and needs. Trust

is essential for both partners to feel safe enough to explore their sexuality without fear of judgment or rejection.

2. Improves Communication
    Emotional intimacy fosters open and honest communication. It makes it easier to express what brings you pleasure and what doesn't, and to navigate any sexual challenges together with respect and care.

3. Creates a Sense of Security
    When you know your partner values you emotionally, you feel more secure in the relationship. This sense of safety allows for deeper sexual exploration and a stronger sense of connection during intimate moments.

4. Promotes Mutual Respect
    Emotional intimacy is built on respect for one another's feelings and needs. When this respect extends into the bedroom, it leads to a more fulfilling sexual relationship where both partners prioritize each other's satisfaction and well-being.

Here are some ways to cultivate emotional intimacy in your relationships, Black women can:

1. Prioritize Open and Honest Communication
    Create a space where you and your partner can openly share your feelings, needs, and desires. Be transparent about your emotional and sexual expectations, and actively listen to your partner's as well.

2. Build Trust Over Time
    Emotional intimacy doesn't happen overnight. It takes time to build trust, so engage in small acts of vulnerability—sharing personal stories, insecurities, or fears—to deepen your bond.

3. Practice Emotional Support
    Emotional intimacy thrives when both partners feel supported. Offer encouragement, be empathetic to your partner's experiences, and seek to understand their emotional needs, just as you would want them to do for you.

4. Engage in Non-Sexual Intimacy
    Emotional closeness grows from everyday gestures of affection and care. Engage in activities like cuddling, talking, or even just spending quality time together to strengthen your bond outside of sex.

5. Seek Professional Guidance if Needed
    If emotional intimacy is difficult to build, don't hesitate to seek therapy or counseling as a couple. Sometimes external guidance is needed to help unpack past traumas or emotional blocks that may be hindering closeness.

When emotional intimacy is nurtured, it deepens the sexual experience, making it more meaningful, satisfying, and joyful. It allows you to show up as your authentic self and experience a connection that goes beyond the physical, fostering a truly healthy and loving sexual relationship.

My hope is you will use these tips to help improve your relationships and support you in becoming comfortable with your sexuality.

When I think about black women being empowered, I think about a black woman who loves herself, her body, and her mind, and understands that her body is her temple and it must be loved, accepted, and respected.

"If we focus on our health, including our inner health, our self-esteem, and how we look at ourselves and our confidence level, we'll tend to be healthier people anyway; we'll tend to make better choices for our lives, for our bodies, we'll always be trying to learn more, and get better as time goes on."
— Queen Latifah, actress and musician

CHAPTER 7

∞

Dynamic Health

*I*n the journey of empowering Black women to live their fullest, most extraordinary lives, the importance of health cannot be overstated. Their bodies are temples, deserving of the utmost care, attention, and respect. In a society where Black women often carry the weight of many roles—whether as mothers, daughters, partners, or leaders—self-care becomes essential, not only for personal well-being but also to be fully present and effective in all areas of life.

Maintaining a healthy weight is a fundamental aspect of physical wellness, but it's about more than aesthetics. It's about honoring your body and safeguarding it against illnesses that disproportionately affect Black women, such as diabetes, heart disease, and high blood pressure. Healthy weight management starts with understanding your body and what it needs. This means finding a balance between eating nourishing foods and staying active, while avoiding extreme diets or unhealthy habits.

Weight can be a sensitive subject, especially for Black women who are often subject to societal pressures around beauty and body image. It's important to approach it with self-love and patience. Focus on health goals that make you feel vibrant and energized rather than pursuing unrealistic ideals. Celebrate your body at every stage of its journey.

Regular exercise is one of the most powerful tools you have for staying healthy and feeling your best. Not only does it help with weight management, but it also strengthens your heart, improves your mood, and boosts energy. Black women face higher risks of conditions like hypertension and cardiovascular disease, and regular physical activity is one of the most effective ways to combat these risks.

You don't have to become a gym enthusiast to stay fit. Whether it's walking, dancing, swimming, or yoga, the key is to find a form of movement that you enjoy. Exercise should never feel like a chore—it's a way to connect with your body, relieve stress, and enhance your overall quality of life. Aim for at least 30 minutes of moderate exercise five days a week. Remember, consistency is more important than intensity.

Food is not just fuel—it's medicine. A balanced, nutrient-rich diet is the cornerstone of good health. As Black women, it's vital to nourish your body with foods that support long-term vitality. Prioritize whole foods like fruits, vegetables, lean proteins, and whole grains while reducing the intake of processed foods, sugar, and unhealthy fats.

Traditional African American cuisine is rich in history, but it's also time to rethink some of the unhealthy habits tied to it. You can still enjoy the foods you love but make healthier choices by baking instead of frying, choosing leaner cuts of meat, and incorporating more vegetables into your meals. Drinking plenty of water and limiting alcohol consumption are also important for maintaining good health.

Stress is an invisible enemy that wreaks havoc on the body and mind. For Black women, who often bear the weight of societal expectations, stress can be even more insidious. Whether it's the pressure of being the backbone of the family or the unique challenges of navigating a world that doesn't always see your worth, chronic stress can take a significant toll on your health.

High levels of stress can contribute to a range of health problems, including hypertension, heart disease, and mental health challenges like anxiety and depression. It's critical to make stress management a priority. Practices like meditation, deep breathing, and mindfulness can help restore balance, as can spending time with loved ones and seeking support when needed. It's not selfish to prioritize your well-being—it's a necessary act of self-preservation.

Heart disease is the leading cause of death for Black women, and two of the most significant risk factors are high blood pressure (hypertension) and high cholesterol. Both of these conditions can be silent—there may be no outward symptoms—so regular monitoring is essential.

Every Black woman should know her blood pressure numbers and cholesterol levels. High blood pressure is known as the "silent killer" because it often goes undetected until serious damage has occurred. Checking these levels regularly allows you to take proactive steps to keep your heart healthy, whether that's through diet, exercise, or medication. Make it a point to discuss your heart health with your doctor during annual checkups.

Preventive care is the foundation of good health. Yet many Black women often neglect regular doctor visits, sometimes due to fear, mistrust of the medical system, or simply being too busy. However, routine checkups are crucial for catching potential health issues before they become major problems.

Annual physical exams should include screenings for conditions like diabetes, cancer, and heart disease, all of which disproportionately affect Black women. You should also discuss your mental health with your healthcare provider. Addressing both physical and mental health in tandem is essential to achieving holistic well-being. Make a commitment to yourself to get that annual checkup—and follow through.

Your health is your most valuable asset. Without it, you can't live the extraordinary life you deserve. As Black women, you are dynamic, powerful, and resilient, but even the strongest among you need to take time to care for their bodies. By watching your weight, staying active, eating nutritious foods, reducing stress, monitoring your heart health, and getting regular checkups, you can maintain the vitality and energy needed to thrive in every aspect of your life.

Remember: self-care is not a luxury; it's a necessity. You are worthy of the time, effort, and care it takes to keep your body and mind healthy. By prioritizing your health, you are giving yourself the greatest gift—the ability to live a long, vibrant, and empowered life.

As Black women, your bodies are more than just physical vessels—they are the sacred temples that carry generations of strength, resilience, and beauty. Yet, in the midst of caring for everyone else, black women often postpone or neglect their own well-being. This chapter is a loving reminder that prioritizing your health isn't selfish—it's necessary.

Studies show that about 4 in 5 Black women are overweight or obese, putting them at higher risk for various health conditions. However, this statistic isn't your destiny.

Understanding and managing your weight begins with:

- Knowing your BMI (Body Mass Index) and healthy weight range
- Setting realistic, achievable weight goals
- Recognizing that healthy bodies come in different shapes and sizes
- Understanding that weight management is about health, not conforming to society's beauty standards

Exercise isn't just about weight loss—it's about celebration of what your bodies can do.

Consider:

- Starting with 30 minutes of moderate activity, 5 days a week
- Finding joy in movement through dance, walking with friends, or community fitness classes
- Incorporating strength training to maintain bone density and muscle mass

- Making exercise social by joining Black women's fitness groups or walking clubs

Healthy eating doesn't mean abandoning our cultural foods. Instead, we can:

- Modify traditional recipes to be healthier while maintaining flavor
- Embrace meal planning to avoid unhealthy convenience foods
- Include more fresh fruits, vegetables, and whole grains
- Stay hydrated with water throughout the day
- Consider consulting with a Black nutritionist who understands our cultural relationship with food

Black women often carry the weight of multiple responsibilities—family, career, community—while navigating systemic racism and gender bias. Managing stress is crucial:

- Practice regular self-care rituals
- Set and maintain healthy boundaries
- Seek therapy or counseling when needed
- Engage in stress-reducing activities like meditation, yoga, or prayer
- Build a support network of other Black women who understand your journey

Regular health monitoring is essential. Key metrics to track include:

- Blood pressure (target: less than 120/80 mmHg)
- Cholesterol levels
- Blood sugar levels
- Body Mass Index (BMI)
- Vitamin D levels (especially important for Black women)

Annual check-ups are non-negotiable. Schedule regular:

- Physical examinations
- Mammograms (starting at age 40, or earlier if family history exists)

- Pap smears
- Dental check-ups
- Eye examinations
- Mental health assessments

The relationship between Black women and the healthcare system is complex, often marked by historical trauma and present-day disparities. To ensure quality care:

- Research and choose healthcare providers who listen to and respect your concerns
- Consider seeking Black healthcare providers who understand your unique health challenges
- Bring a trusted friend or family member to appointments if needed
- Keep detailed health records
- Don't hesitate to seek second opinions

Health transformation is more sustainable with support.

Consider:

- Joining health-focused Black women's groups
- Finding an accountability partner for fitness goals
- Connecting with health-conscious friends for meal prep sessions
- Sharing health information and resources within your community

Remember that taking care of your health is an act of self-love and resistance. When you prioritize your well-being, you:

- Set an example for future generations
- Honor the sacrifices of those who came before us
- Create space for joy and longevity
- Demonstrate that Black women's health matters

1. Schedule your annual check-up if you haven't already
2. Start a health journal to track your metrics
3. Create a realistic exercise plan that brings you joy

4. Develop a stress management routine
5. Connect with other Black women on their health journeys
6. Make a list of your health goals and display them prominently

Your health journey is uniquely yours, but you're not alone. As Black women, when you take care of yourself, you contribute to the collective healing and empowerment of our community. Your body is a testament to generations of strength—honor it, nurture it, and watch it flourish.

Naming and honoring that which is holy in our body-temple makes us God on the earth. We are human expressions of the divine. We are not territory to be conquered. We are God's Good Creation, meant to be cherished.

— Lyvonne Briggs

CHAPTER 8

Spirituality

$\mathcal{T}$hroughout history, Black women have been the bedrock of resilience, faith, and hope for our communities. In the face of unimaginable suffering—slavery, segregation, systemic oppression, and countless other atrocities—religion became a source of strength and survival. For generations, the church served not only as a place of worship but as a refuge, a place to gather, to organize, and to heal. It offered solace and gave meaning to suffering, allowing Black women to keep going even when the world seemed stacked against them.

But we are living in a time of great transformation. While traditional religion has been the foundation that kept us grounded, there is a new spiritual awakening happening across the globe. Reports suggest that people, especially within the Black community, are leaving organized religion in droves. But if we look closer, what we are witnessing is not the abandonment of faith; rather, it is a shift. People aren't losing their connection to the divine—they are deepening it, seeking new ways to connect that go beyond the walls of a church, mosque, or synagogue.

There is no denying the role Christianity has played in helping Black women survive the cruelties of this country. The Bible's promises of a better future, of justice and salvation, provided comfort in the face of relentless injustice. The church was often the only institution where Black women could express their full humanity and feel empowered. The hymns, prayers, and scriptures became the language of resistance, hope, and inner strength. For many Black women, the church offered the only space where their souls could rest and recharge.

But as we move further into the 21st century, we must also recognize that the spiritual journey is evolving. Black women today are more open-minded and spiritually curious than ever before. They are beginning to understand that while religion offered us survival tools, spirituality can offer us a deeper, more intimate connection with the divine—one that is not bound by dogma, tradition, or the interpretations of others.

To truly love yourself as a Black woman, and to embrace your full potential, it's important to realize that your relationship with God does not have to be confined to any one religion. The divine is far greater than any single tradition. And as we evolve, so too must our understanding of what it means to be spiritual.

More and more Black women are seeking personal spiritual experiences. They are learning to meditate, practice mindfulness, explore ancient African spiritual traditions, and embrace New Thought philosophies that focus on the power of the mind to create reality. The beauty of this moment is that they are no longer allowing themselves to be defined outdated interpretations about God. Instead, they are seeking and finding their own truth.

Spirituality is not about abandoning your past or rejecting religion. For many Black women, Christianity will always hold a special place in their hearts. But this new spiritual journey is about expanding the ways they connect with God and with themselves. It's about realizing that there are countless ways to feel divine love, and none of them require a specific denomination, building, or preacher to validate them.

The decline in organized religion should not be seen as a crisis, but rather a shift toward individual empowerment. We are living in a time when people want more direct experiences with the divine. We are no longer satisfied with someone telling us how to believe or what to believe. We want to feel God for ourselves, in our own way.

Black women, in particular, are embracing this shift. they are recognizing that spiritual practices such as yoga, meditation, and ancestral veneration can complement their Christian faith—or, for some, replace it altogether. The essence of this movement is simple: it's about finding the divine within. It's about understanding that the spark of God lives inside each and every one of us, and we have the power to nurture and grow that connection on our own terms.

Despite what the headlines may say, Black women are not turning away from faith. They are simply expanding our spiritual horizons. They are understanding that their spiritual journey is not about fear or judgment but about love, inner peace, and healing. It's about creating a personal relationship with the divine that uplifts you and empowers you to be the queen that you are.

This shift toward spirituality doesn't mean that religion is obsolete. For many, religion will continue to be a source of community, structure, and meaning. But we can no longer ignore the fact that many Black women are searching for something deeper—something that aligns with their personal experiences and truths.

We are waking up to the fact that spirituality is not a one-size-fits-all journey. Some will continue to find comfort in church pews, while others will discover the divine in nature, in stillness, or in the ancient wisdom of our ancestors. And all of these paths are valid. The key is to remain open to the possibility that God can be found in a variety of ways and places.

As Black women, they have always been spiritually resilient. It's in their DNA. But now, they are embracing a new kind of freedom—the freedom to explore their spirituality without fear, without limits, and without judgment. Whether through prayer, meditation, or simply being present in the moment, they are finding ways to connect with the divine that resonate with their souls.

The time has come for them to trust themselves and their own experiences. The time has come to understand that their spiritual journey is personal, powerful, and ever-evolving. And in this new age of spiritual awakening, Black women are leading the way, discovering new depths of faith and divine love. Let us continue to embrace this path with open hearts, knowing that our connection to the divine is as limitless as we allow it to be.

In this new era, Black women are stepping into their spiritual power. They are becoming the architects of their own divine connection. Whether through organized religion, personal spiritual practices, or a combination of both, the path to God is theirs to define. What matters most is not where or how they worship, but that they nurture a relationship with the divine that uplifts, strengthens, and empowers them to live their fullest lives.

And in this journey, they are not alone. As Black women, they carry within them the wisdom of our ancestors and the courage of our foremothers. Let us continue to walk this path with grace, knowing that we are loved, guided, and supported by a divine power far greater than any single religion could ever contain.

To the Black women reading this: your spiritual journey is valid, whether it leads you to a church altar or a meditation cushion. The divine force that guided our ancestors knows no boundaries and isn't limited to any single tradition. Your truth may lie in the familiar comfort of traditional religious practice, in the exploration of alternative spiritual paths, or in a combination that's uniquely your own.

The time has come to embrace this spiritual expansion with the same courage our forebears showed in holding onto their faith through the darkest of times. We can honor their legacy not by limiting ourselves to their exact practices, but by maintaining their unwavering commitment to spiritual truth while being open to new ways of connecting with the divine.

Remember, spirituality is not about following a prescribed path—it's about finding the way that brings you closest to your higher power. As Black women, you carry within you the spiritual strength of generations. Now, you have the freedom to express that strength in ways that resonate with your individual souls while remaining connected to your collective spiritual heritage.

Your journey to the divine is as unique as your fingerprint, and that's exactly as it should be. Trust your spirit to guide you to your truth, whether that leads you to a traditional church, a meditation center, or your own sacred space of spiritual discovery.

As a former atheist, there was a time in my life when I was absolutely convinced God did not exist. I decided to rely on science and facts to guide me through life. After being a confirmed atheist for several years, something was missing. I couldn't really explain it, but there was a void inside of me that science couldn't fill. So, I decided to go on a journey to figure out how to fill that void. I started by researching the major religions of the world. I went to a Buddhist temple, learned about their beliefs, and had some very deep discussions about what they believed. I went to a Muslim mosque and learned some interesting things about Islam and their beliefs. I visited a Jewish synagogue and learned about the Torah and how it was tied to Christianity. I went to a Hindu temple and was blown away by their belief in multiple gods.

After a few years of research, I came to the conclusion that they all were basically saying the same thing. They all pointed to a simple truth: there is a power greater than us in the universe, and we all have direct access to this power. That power goes by many different names, but each religion was designed to give you access to that power.

After coming to that conclusion, I was able to change my mind about being an atheist, and I committed to finding my truth about God. It was an interesting journey, which began with me learning how to meditate. It was through meditation that I began to accept there was this higher power that I had access to, and the way to access it was through my mind and heart. When I finally learned to listen to and trust my own heart, I realized why I didn't believe in God in the first place. I didn't believe in God because I was trying to find God through my mind and intellect, and God simply did not make sense to me. It wasn't until I allowed myself to feel and experience God in my heart that I was able to know God intimately. I learned that I could not experience God in my head; I had to feel it in my heart.

By developing an intimacy and connection with this higher power, it has allowed me to not just believe God exists, but to intimately know that God exists. It has been an amazing journey, and it is my connection to this higher power that drives me to do my part in helping make the world a better place.

I'd like to close this chapter on spirituality by sharing a chapter from my book *What If Jesus Were A Coach*. It will explain how I came to my conclusions about God and hopefully provide you with some insights that help you develop an intimacy and connection with your higher power.

"Growing up as a child, I remember the picture of Jesus hanging up in my grandparents' home. It was the familiar picture of the white Jesus with a light emanating from his heart, symbolizing his love for humanity. I also remember the Jesus nailed on the cross wall-hanging sculpture which also adorned their walls. Even as a child, I didn't understand why Jesus was white, and why he seemed to hate Black people so much.

You see, my grandparents were extremely religious even though they never went to church. As I mentioned in the previous chapter, they forced me to go to church, yet they never attended. This definitely caused some major conflicts in my mind because even though they talked a lot about Jesus, their actions did not reflect Jesus' teachings. My grandmother was a raging alcoholic who physically and verbally abused me. How could I follow Jesus when the grown-up responsible for raising me was such a terrible person?

On the other hand, my grandfather was a quiet gentleman who was deeply religious and filled with wisdom. Even though he only had an eighth-grade education, he was one of the smartest men I've ever known. Some of my fondest memories from childhood were having conversations with him about just anything. We would sit outside in the yard amongst a myriad of farm animals, and he would share stories about a wide variety of topics, including life. Even though I was just a kid, he talked to me as though I was much older, and he challenged me to always think about things very deeply.

One day, I asked him why God was so angry at Black people. This was during the civil rights movement, as I watched news stories of Black people being attacked by dogs, sprayed with fire hoses, and beaten by cops. My young ten-year-old mind couldn't understand why Black people were so maltreated. So, in my mind, I concluded that Black people must have done something really bad since Jesus didn't step in and stop the abuse they were enduring.

When I asked the question, he picked up on the sadness and fear in my voice, and he lifted me and placed me on his knee. He then told me that God wasn't angry at Black people. He said that God had a perfect plan, and even though we may not fully understand it, God's plan was perfect. But how could God's plan be so perfect while Black people were being so mistreated?

He told me not to worry and to trust the divine plan of God.

As a ten-year-old, I couldn't fully understand what he meant. I tried to rationalize how God's plan was perfect, but I just couldn't see it. In retrospect, and as an adult now, I can definitely understand the perfection of the plan he was talking about. Still, it has taken me years of deep self-introspection and research to fully grasp the implications of what my grandfather told me.

I'm reminded of a quote by Albert Einstein that says, "If you can't explain your subject to an eighth-grader, you don't fully understand your topic." With that being said, I'd like to share how I now see God and how I came to my understanding.

First of all, I think most people see God as this anthropomorphic being that resides up in heaven somewhere. Since most people in the West are Christians, they have this common view that God is some old guy in the clouds who is taking notes on their lives and waiting for them to "sin" so he can banish them to eternal damnation in a fiery hell. This is one of the most erroneous teachings of most organized Western religions. The error is thinking and believing that God is a human being just like us. Since God is just like us, he must have human emotions and needs, and therefore organized religions have built an entire theology based on the idea that God acts like a human. Why else would "he" create the Ten Commandments? Why else would we have to prove our love for him so he wouldn't punish us? Does it make sense to you that an omniscient and omnipresent God would get angry at you for making mistakes? Does it make sense to you that God is a jealous God? These things do not make sense to me, which is why I've always had an issue with organized religion.

The reason most people see God as a human being can be traced to Genesis 1:27, where it says, "So God created man in his own image, in the image of God he created him; male and female he created them." This verse has been misinterpreted, and most religions have concluded that this passage implies that God looks like a human being.

But if you read John 4:24, it should clarify who and what God is. It says, "God is spirit, and his worshipers must worship in the Spirit and in truth." As it says, "God is spirit," and since we were made in the image and after the likeness of God, that means we are spirit also.

According to Dr. Wayne Dyer (author and spiritual teacher), we are not human beings having a spiritual experience; we are spiritual beings having a human experience. If you can embrace this idea, rest assured this book will make a lot more sense.

Since most people see Jesus as the personification of God in human form, they have accepted this erroneous belief that God must think and act just like a human being. This is the origin of most conflicts in the world—believing that God is a "someone" instead of a "something." It is my belief that God is the Divine Intelligence that created and is still creating this amazing universe we live in. Therefore, I see God as more of a "what" than a "who." Seeing God this way answers another question I had as a child: Where was God before the universe began?

To answer that question, let's begin by listening to two of the most brilliant men and greatest minds the world has ever seen.

Albert Einstein once said, "Everything is energy, that's just the way that it is. Match the frequency of the reality you want to create, and there is no way you can't create that reality. It can be no other way. This isn't philosophy, this is physics."

Nikola Tesla said, "If you want to understand the universe, you must think in terms of energy, frequency, and vibration."

Both of these brilliant minds point to a scientific fact: everything is energy! So, where did this energy come from? This is the million-dollar question!

To answer it, you basically have three options:

Option 1: It was a random act that just happened. Option 2: Something caused it to happen. Option 3: You do not know where it came from.

Option number one is based on science. Science says there was a Big Bang that occurred randomly, and the universe is the result of a chemical reaction that evolved into our current universe.

Option number two is based on a belief that a Creator caused the universe to take form. Every religion is based on this option.

Option number three is, "I really do not know!"

So, which option best describes what you believe? Option #1, Option #2, or Option #3?

To help you choose which option you believe, let's go back several thousand years. Try to imagine what it must have been like to be a caveman. During that time, your primary responsibility was to provide food and shelter for yourself and your family and protect them from being eaten alive by dangerous animals (though not dinosaurs, as humans and dinosaurs did not coexist). For the most part, it was a simple life. You didn't have language, but you learned to communicate with pictures and sounds. As cave dwellers evolved, they developed language and learned to make weapons and basic tools for survival. As they continued to evolve, they encountered certain things they didn't understand or have control over, so they came up with stories and ideas to make sense of natural phenomena. For example, when lightning struck, they had no idea where it came from, so they created stories to explain its origin. They then came up with the idea that some sort of powerful force in the sky was shooting lightning bolts at them. If they contracted a disease, they created stories that said the gods in the sky were angry and were punishing them. So, it was humankind's lack of understanding of the physical world that caused them to create explanations for things they didn't understand. Therefore, these stories became religions.

As these stories were passed down from generation to generation, humans were still evolving. Some highly evolved beings began teaching that there was a Creator of all things, and they provided new stories about how this Creator operated. These evolved beings laid the groundwork for all religions, and their teachings spread across the globe.

The problem, as I see it, is that each of these evolved beings shared a message of oneness with the Creator. However, each evolved being had their unique interpretation of what the Creator expected from humans, and they shared their "truth" with the masses. The masses, in turn, began sharing those truths with others. Unfortunately, many of the evolved beings' messages were lost in translation, misinterpreted, or even completely changed. Yet the masses concluded that their evolved being was the chosen one, and if you didn't follow their evolved being's way of worshipping God, you couldn't be a part of their tribe. Each tribe believed their evolved being was teaching the "right" way to connect with God, while other evolved beings were teaching the "wrong" way.

Therefore, religion is a belief in the story of an evolved being who came to teach humans how to connect to the Creator. The downside of religion is that it promotes exclusivity. If you do not believe in their teachings, you are seen as different and separate from that particular group. In other words, if you do not believe in what they believe, you cannot be a part of their tribe. This is the core essence of religion.

On the other hand, there is spirituality. Spirituality suggests that several evolved beings have walked the earth, each sharing the same message: that there is a Divine Creator of the Universe, and every human being has equal access to this Creator. Being spiritual but not religious means recognizing that all religions originate from the same source and lead to the same place. Therefore, you accept that some people may believe in a different God than yours, but that doesn't mean they can't be a part of your tribe. Spirituality is all-inclusive and welcomes all humans into one universal tribe.

There was a time when I believed in option #1. As I mentioned earlier, I concluded that there was no such thing as God, and I held firm to the belief that science had the answer to everything. If it couldn't be proven by science, it simply wasn't real. But then I made a paradigm shift. I changed my rigid way of thinking by researching different religions and coming to my own conclusions and beliefs about God.

To provide you with some fuel for contemplation, I'd like to share some things I've learned that confirm for me that science and spirituality actually go together. I realize that some people may not believe this, but I assume you are open-minded enough to consider what I'm about to share since you're still reading. Let's go back to the quote, "everything is energy." There is a scientific process called reductionism, which means you can take anything and reduce it down to its smallest component to know exactly what it is made of. There was a time when scientists thought the smallest particle of matter was the atom, so they concluded that the atom was the building block of all matter. As science evolved and technology improved, they realized the atom wasn't the smallest particle of matter.

When they broke everything down into its smallest component, they discovered that everything was composed of energy. In other words, nothing is actually solid. It's energy vibrating at different speeds, and as this energy slows down, it becomes solid matter. Dr. Joe Dispenza explained it this way: "If you stripped an atom down to its raw essentials, all that exists is energy and information, but the atom is not without design. Even at that quantum level, there exists a structure and orderliness, so there must be some intelligence or force that is unifying and ordering them." So, what is this intelligence or force, and where did it come from?

Once again, this is the million-dollar question. Did this energy and intelligence randomly appear, or did "something" cause it to appear? As a result of my own research, I have come to conclusions that I would like to share with you. To fully grasp what I'm about to share, it may require you to create a new paradigm regarding how the Universe began.

I'd like you to try to imagine complete darkness and emptiness. Put another way, try to imagine complete nothingness. In this nothingness, nothing exists. There is no light or darkness, not even time. It is pure nothingness. Can you imagine it? Now try to imagine that all of a sudden, something came from nothing. If you believe in science, the moment something came from nothing was called the Big Bang.

If you're religious, it was in that moment that God said, "Let there be light." Either way, the point is that at first, there was nothing, and then there was something. If you choose to see this event from a scientific perspective, how would you explain that? If there was absolute nothingness and then something came from nothing, that means the nothingness was actually something because it would be impossible for something to come from nothing. Are you still with me? Think deeply about that. How could something come from nothing? I would like to propose that the nothingness is actually something, and that something could be called Pure Consciousness or Divine Intelligence. You could even call it Love, which is the highest vibration in the Universe. If you're religious, you can call it God. As I see it, it is the Source of all things. Everything in the Universe arises from this Divine Intelligence. The moment something came from nothing, an energy was released, and an intelligence drives this energy. The intelligence that drives this energy is called evolution. Evolution is the process through which Divine Intelligence evolves to deeper and deeper levels of complexity, and this is an ongoing process that will continue throughout eternity.

This energy is within you, and true spirituality is developing an intimacy and connection with this energy. You do not have to be religious to connect to this energy. Even if you do not believe in this energy, it is still there. Each religion is supposed to help you recognize this energy within you. Unfortunately, most religions get caught up in religious dogma and doctrine and fail to teach you the truth of accessing this energy.

This answers my question of where God was before the Universe began. God was everywhere because God is everything. If God were a human being, where would he/she have been before the Universe began? Hmmm?

I do not believe we can fully grasp exactly what God is in our limited human minds. By choosing to see God as Love, Divine Intelligence, or Pure Consciousness, we can grasp the idea of God, though it doesn't fully explain what God truly is. It's like trying to imagine how long eternity is. Eternity is forever. It never stops. So is God; it is everything and nothing at the same time. It doesn't come to an end. Now that I've shared how I see God, I'd like to share something else I've learned about God and the Holy Trinity. Have you ever had someone try to explain the Holy Trinity to you? The Trinity states that there is The Father, The Son, and The Holy Spirit, yet they are all supposed to be the same thing. How is that possible? This is incredibly confusing, and I definitely had difficulty understanding it based on traditional Christianity. So, I would like to share my perception of the Holy Trinity.

To start, let's take a look at Genesis Chapter 1, verse 26. "Then God said, 'Let us make man in our image, in our likeness, and let them rule over the fish of the sea and the birds of the air, over the livestock, over all the earth, and over all the creatures that move along the ground.'" Let me preface this explanation with a little caveat: I do not believe in the literal interpretation of the Bible. I believe in the metaphysical interpretation. This means the stories in the Bible are metaphorical, allegorical, and not written to be taken literally, but rather to be understood spiritually and metaphorically. Therefore, each story provides us with an opportunity to learn something about ourselves to help us grow into the best version of ourselves.

One question I could never get a minister to answer was based on that quote from Genesis 1:26. Why did God say, "Let 'us' make man in 'our' image?" Who was he referring to when he said that? Why didn't he say, "Let me make man in my image?" I've never had anyone explain this to me so I'm certain someone reading this has the same question. Now I'd like to share my answer. Let's go back to the beginning. Remember when I said there was nothing, and then all of a sudden, there was something? The nothingness was God or Pure Consciousness. The instant something came from nothing, something was "born." That something which was born could be referred to as an energy. Since the Bible was written by men from a patriarchal point of view, we use the term "Father," but in reality, "Mother" would have been more appropriate since men do not give birth. However, for the sake of this discussion, we will leave that aside. So, the "Father," which is God or Divine Intelligence, gave birth to an energy which we will call its son. If you practice Christianity, you would call this son Christ. If you follow the Tao, you would call this son Chi, and if you're Native American, you would call this son Catori.

Regardless of what you call it, it is an energy that originated from the Father or Creator. So now you have the Father and the Son, but what about the Holy Spirit? The Holy Spirit is the individual expression of the Son. Think of it this way: there is a spark of divinity in every human being. You have it, I have it, everyone has it. This spark, this energy, is divine, and it is your birthright. This spark, which was birthed by the Father and expressed by the Son, needed a way to be expressed, so God created man/woman to be the divine expression of itself.

Here is a simple story to illustrate what I mean:

Once upon a time, God was sitting up in heaven looking down at the earth at human beings with a few of his angels when he became overwhelmed with pride. "Human beings are without question my greatest creations. I want to give them something that I didn't give to any other creatures on earth; I want to give them a part of me. But I don't want to just give it to them; I want them to earn it so they will truly appreciate this divine gift. So, I need to figure out a place to put it where they will have to put forth some effort to find it. Where do you think I should put it?"

One of the angels spoke up and said, "I know where you can put it. Why not put it on top of the tallest mountain?" God thought about it for a moment, and then he said, "I don't think that's a good idea. Human beings will easily climb the highest mountain and find this gift." Then another angel spoke up, "I know where to hide it. Why not put it at the bottom of the ocean? Surely it would be difficult for man to find it there." Once again, God thought about it and said, "I don't think so. Human beings are naturally curious, and I don't think they would have any problem finding it at the bottom of the ocean."

Then another angel spoke up, "Why not place it amongst the stars? Surely human beings would find it difficult to find among the stars." God pondered the idea for a moment and responded the same way. "Human beings are ingenious and adventurous. I don't think it would be hard for them to find it among the stars."

Then another angel walked up to God and said, "I know the perfect place for you to hide it. I am certain it would be the last place human beings would ever look. Why not put your divine spark inside of them?" All of a sudden, a huge smile came across God's face. "That is brilliant! What a great idea. I agree with you totally, so I will place my divine spark inside every human being, and it will be up to them to find it."

This story serves as a perfect metaphor for what the Holy Spirit is. It is a divine spark of God, which gives us access to God in our own unique, individual way, and it is our responsibility to find it. No one can find it for us. One of my favorite quotes is, "If you don't go within, you will always go without." Therefore, if you are unwilling to look within your own heart and mind, you will never find God. Most religions have promoted the idea that God is somewhere outside of you, but the truth is, God has always been inside of you.

Going back to the story I shared about God looking down on earth at human beings and being proud of his creations, God came up with the perfect plan to find a way to express itself on earth. In Genesis 1:27, it says, "So God created man in his own image, in the image of God he created him; male and female he created them." Verse 28 says, "God blessed them and said to them: Be fruitful and multiply; fill the earth and subdue it. Rule over the fish of the sea and the birds of the air and over every living creature that moves on the ground." The way I interpret those two verses is that God made it clear that human beings were its greatest creation. They were given a divine part of God, and therefore, they had dominion over all other creations. Looking at it from a metaphysical perspective, human beings are divine individual expressions of God.

Think of it this way:

Take a moment and think about the ocean. If you stand on a beach and look toward the horizon, it looks infinite, beautiful, powerful, and majestic. Now imagine that you have a jar, and you walk to the ocean and scoop up a jar of water. The jar of water has the exact same qualities, characteristics, and attributes of the ocean. It is, in fact, the ocean. There is no difference. But can the jar of water be the ocean in its totality? No! It is an individual expression of the ocean, but it cannot be the entire ocean. And yet, there is absolutely no difference.

This is another way to see God. God is the ocean, and you are an individual expression of God. You have all of the same qualities, characteristics, and attributes of God, but you could never be God in totality.

Put another way, you are a divine personality in the mind of God. As personalities in the mind of God, God communicates with us through divine ideas. Ideas are the currency of the Universe, and when you learn to quiet the noise of your mind and move into the silence of your heart, then you will hear the voice of your soul, which are the divine ideas that come directly from God.

I'd like to close this chapter with a very important question. As a matter of fact, it's possibly the most important question you've ever been asked. So, when I ask the question, I want you to take a moment and truly think about it before you answer. Spend some time in deep contemplation, and then answer the question as honestly as you can.

Try not to allow other people's opinions or what you have been taught to believe to influence your answer. Listen to your own heart and mind and answer truthfully. No one needs to know your answer except you. Are you ready?

What are your beliefs about God?

Notice I didn't ask if you believe in God; I asked what your beliefs about God are. Some people may not believe God exists, while others may have a very strong belief in God. Some may envision an anthropomorphic god sitting in heaven, taking notes on their lives and waiting to see if they are worthy of entering heaven. Others may believe in a God of love who embraces them unconditionally, accepting them with open, loving arms and showering them with grace.

If you truly want to know what type of God you believe in, let me suggest you simply take a deep look at your life right now, and you will find your answer. Always remember, your belief about something creates your experience of it. If you believe in an angry, judgmental God to whom you must repent for your sins in order to get into heaven, chances are your life is filled with fear and anxiety.

On the other hand, if you believe in a God of love, your life may be filled with joy, inner peace, and happiness. Ultimately, your beliefs about God will always shape your experience of God, so it's important to be really clear about what you believe. I am convinced that most people don't truly know what they believe about God. They may know what they were taught to believe through their families and cultures, but they have never really questioned or challenged those beliefs. They have simply accepted beliefs passed down for generations and are absolutely convinced that their beliefs are the "right" ones, and anyone who doesn't share them is "wrong."

It is now up to you to decide how you see God. I hope this chapter has provided you with some fuel for contemplation and some insights that will support you in creating an intimate connection with a power greater than yourself.

Rest assured, when you do, your life will become miraculous!

"Be brave enough to live life creatively. The creative is the place where no one else has ever been. You have to leave the city of your comfort and go into the wilderness of your intuition. You can't get there by bus, only by hard work and risk and by not quite knowing what you're doing. What you'll discover will be wonderful. What you'll discover will be yourself.
— Carla Harris

CHAPTER 9

Abundance

Abundance is a state of mind. It begins not with the material wealth you hold in your hands, but with the beliefs you carry in your heart and the thoughts that fill your mind. For Black women, who have long stood at the intersection of racial and gender struggles, understanding the spiritual power of mindset is crucial to not only survival but to thriving in a world that often seems designed to limit their potential. Yet, within each of us is the power to shift our reality and attract abundance—wealth, success, and fulfillment—by transforming the way we think.

Wealth isn't just about money. It is about living a life full of joy, purpose, and satisfaction. At its core, abundance is a spiritual concept. It arises from the belief that the universe is infinitely generous, and it flows to those who open themselves to receive. This is not a passive act but a deliberate choice to cultivate thoughts that align with abundance, rather than scarcity.

Scarcity, by contrast, is rooted in fear—the fear of not having enough, not being enough, or losing what little you have. For generations, Black women have been conditioned to operate in this space due to societal limitations placed upon them. However, as we evolve, we must recognize that these are external barriers, and the true limitation often lies in our minds. Shifting from a scarcity mindset to an abundance mindset is the first step toward manifesting the wealth and success we desire.

The power of thought cannot be overstated. Our thoughts shape our beliefs, our actions, and ultimately our reality. When we focus on lack—whether it's money, opportunities, or love—we attract more lack. But when we align our thoughts with abundance, we become magnets for prosperity. This is the essence of the law of attraction, a spiritual principle that teaches us that like attracts like.

If you believe that you are deserving of abundance, you will begin to see opportunities where none seemed to exist before. If you consistently think thoughts of prosperity, wealth will find its way to you. The universe responds to the frequency of your thoughts, and when you think in terms of abundance, you vibrate at a higher frequency that attracts abundance in return.

For Black women, changing the narrative about wealth and abundance is a revolutionary act. They are taught to be humble, to expect little, and to be content with what they have, even when it isn't enough. But to embrace abundance, we must reject the belief that we should "settle" or that we are destined for struggle. Wealth is not reserved for someone else; it is our birthright, but we must first believe that to be true.

Consider the women who have risen against all odds to create wealth— not just in terms of finances, but in their relationships, health, and personal fulfillment. Their stories are not just stories of hard work but of mental and spiritual alignment. They shifted their mindset from one of scarcity to one of abundance. They believed they were worthy of more, and as a result, they created more.

So how do you cultivate an abundance mindset? The journey begins with awareness. Pay attention to your thoughts. How often do you think about what you don't have? How often do you focus on lack or fear? Shift your focus. Start by practicing gratitude for what you do have, no matter how small it may seem. Gratitude is the foundation of abundance because it shifts your energy from fear to appreciation, from scarcity to fullness.

Next, visualize your wealth. See yourself living the life of abundance you desire. Picture yourself with financial freedom, healthy relationships, and a deep sense of purpose. The more vividly you can see it, the more real it becomes in your mind, and eventually in your reality.

Finally, speak abundance into existence. The words you use carry power. Speak affirmations that reinforce your abundance mindset. Say things like, "I am worthy of wealth," "Opportunities are everywhere," and "I am a magnet for prosperity." These words, spoken with conviction, shift your internal narrative and open the floodgates to wealth.

While mindset is the key to abundance, it must be paired with action. However, the actions you take when operating from an abundance mindset are different from those driven by fear. When you believe that the universe is on your side, you are willing to take risks, to pursue opportunities, and to invest in your dreams. Inspired action comes from a place of confidence and trust that everything you need will be provided.

Remember that abundance is about more than money—it's about having the freedom to live on your terms. For Black women, abundance is about dismantling the generational limitations placed on them and creating new legacies of wealth, power, and influence for ourselves and future generations.

The journey to abundance starts in your mind. It's about embracing a spiritual understanding that the universe is generous, and you are deserving of its gifts. Black women have the power to reshape their narratives, align their thoughts with wealth, and take inspired actions to attract prosperity into their lives. By shifting from a scarcity mindset to one of abundance, we not only change our lives but also the world around us.

Abundance is your birthright—claim it.

Building Financial Wealth

Financial freedom is one of the most empowering achievements anyone can attain, and for Black women, it is a critical tool for creating a life of independence, security, and opportunity. Historically, Black women have faced unique economic challenges, but today, more than ever, they have the ability to overcome those obstacles and build lasting wealth. In this section, we will explore practical tips and strategies to help you achieve financial freedom, focusing on the key pillars of saving, maintaining a good credit score, and investing.

Saving money is the foundation of wealth-building. It's not about how much money you make, but how much you keep and grow over time. Having a strong savings habit not only provides financial security in times of uncertainty but also opens the door to investment opportunities that can generate future wealth.

One of the most effective ways to save is to "pay yourself first." This means setting aside a portion of your income as soon as you receive it. Whether it's 10% or 20%, automate your savings so that it happens without you having to think about it. This ensures that you are consistently building your financial cushion. Additionally, having an emergency fund with at least three to six months' worth of living expenses is crucial for weathering financial setbacks like job loss or medical emergencies.

To make saving easier, create a budget. This helps you track your income and expenses, making it clear where your money is going and where you can cut back to increase your savings. As a Black woman striving for financial independence, budgeting can also empower you to prioritize spending on things that truly matter while eliminating wasteful spending.

Your credit score is one of the most powerful financial tools you can have. It determines your ability to borrow money, the interest rates you receive, and even your eligibility for certain jobs and housing. A good credit score opens doors to financial opportunities, while a poor one can close them. For this reason, understanding and managing your credit score should be a top priority in your wealth-building journey.

A good credit score, typically above 700, signals to lenders that you are a responsible borrower, making it easier for you to qualify for loans and credit cards with favorable terms. To build and maintain a strong credit score, focus on paying your bills on time, keeping your credit card balances low, and not opening too many new accounts at once.

One of the key strategies to improve your credit score is to reduce credit card debt. High credit card balances negatively impact your credit utilization ratio, which is a major factor in your score. Aim to keep your credit utilization below 30% of your available credit limit.

Regularly checking your credit report is another important habit. You're entitled to a free credit report every year from the major credit bureaus, and reviewing it can help you spot any errors or fraudulent activity that could be dragging down your score. A good credit score is essential not only for borrowing but also for securing lower insurance rates and even impressing potential employers.

While saving and maintaining good credit are essential steps in building financial wealth, investing is what truly accelerates your financial growth. Investing allows your money to work for you, generating more wealth over time. The earlier you start, the more time your money has to grow, thanks to the power of compound interest.

There are several ways to invest, including stocks, bonds, real estate, and retirement accounts like 401(k)s and IRAs. If you're new to investing, a great place to start is with your employer's retirement plan, especially if they offer a matching contribution. This is essentially free money that can compound over time, significantly increasing your retirement savings.

Diversification is another important principle of investing. This means spreading your investments across different asset classes to reduce risk. For example, you could invest in stocks, which offer higher returns but come with more risk, and balance them with bonds, which are more stable but offer lower returns. Real estate is also a great investment option, as it can provide both income and long-term appreciation.

For Black women, investing is not just about building wealth—it's about creating generational wealth. When you invest wisely, you create opportunities not just for yourself, but for your children and future generations. It's important to educate yourself on different investment strategies and, if necessary, seek advice from a financial advisor who can help you tailor a plan that aligns with your financial goals.

Building financial wealth requires discipline, education, and long-term planning. It is important to set clear financial goals—whether that's buying a home, retiring early, or starting a business—and to create a plan to achieve them. By combining consistent saving, maintaining a strong credit score, and investing, you can move from financial uncertainty to financial freedom.

But it's also important to remember that building wealth is about more than just money. It's about creating a life of freedom, choice, and security. As Black women, financial freedom allows you to step into your power and live life on your own terms, without depending on anyone else for our livelihood.

Financial freedom is within your reach. By developing the habit of saving, maintaining a good credit score, and learning to invest wisely, you can build a foundation of wealth that will not only serve you but also the generations that follow. As you embark on this journey, remember that financial empowerment is about more than just accumulating money—it's about taking control of your future, creating opportunities, and leaving a lasting legacy. You deserve financial abundance, and with the right mindset and strategies, you can achieve it.

"The success of every woman should be the inspiration to another. We should raise each other up. Make sure you're very courageous: be strong, be extremely kind, and above all be humble."
— Serena Williams

CHAPTER 10

Service

*M*uhammad Ali, one of the greatest athletes and humanitarians of all time, once said, "Being in service is the rent we pay for our time here on earth." This profound statement captures the essence of what it means to live a life of purpose—recognizing that our gifts, talents, and abilities are not just for personal gain, but meant to uplift others and leave a positive mark on the world.

In today's society, it can be easy to get caught up in the pursuit of personal success, financial wealth, and individual recognition. While these aspirations are important, they must be balanced with a deeper understanding of service to humanity. For Black men and women, especially, this calling to serve takes on a unique significance. Our collective history is filled with resilience, perseverance, and the constant striving for better lives not just for ourselves but for future generations. Service has always been at the core of that journey.

Each of us is born with a set of unique gifts and talents. These may be artistic, intellectual, athletic, or interpersonal. Whatever form they take, they represent a piece of our individuality that we can offer to the world. To truly be in service is to recognize these gifts, develop them, and then use them to improve the lives of others. Whether it is through mentoring, teaching, creating, or leading, your contribution to humanity is tied to the authentic expression of who you are.

When we share our gifts with the world, we inspire others to do the same. We become examples of what it means to live a fulfilled life—one rooted in purpose, passion, and contribution. Black women, especially, have long been the backbone of their families and communities, often in ways that go unnoticed or undervalued. From nurturing the next generation to leading movements for social change, Black women have consistently shown the world the power of service.

To serve others is, at its core, an act of love. Love for humanity, love for community, and love for the future. Service is the bridge that connects our individual strengths to the collective well-being of those around us. When Black men and women commit to serving one another, we create a ripple effect that strengthens our families, our communities, and our culture.

One of the greatest acts of service is the willingness to uplift and support each other in times of need. Whether through mentorship, financial assistance, or emotional support, service can take many forms. By fostering a spirit of service within our families and communities, we build stronger bonds that help us overcome adversity and celebrate success together. We create a legacy of care, compassion, and collaboration that future generations will carry forward.

It's important to recognize that service extends beyond just the people we know personally. It is about being in service to humanity as a whole. Whether we are advocating for social justice, working to close economic gaps, or simply being kind to strangers, service in all its forms contributes to a better world.

Service doesn't have to be grand or global to make a difference. It can be as simple as being present for a friend in need, volunteering at a local organization, or using your platform to amplify marginalized voices. No matter how large or small, every act of service counts.

In a world that often glorifies individualism, it's crucial to remember that true fulfillment comes not just from personal achievement but from how we impact the lives of others. The joy and satisfaction that come from giving of ourselves far outweigh any material gains. Service reminds us that we are all interconnected, and our greatest purpose is to lift one another up.

Black men and women have a rich history of service, from civil rights leaders to educators, artists, and entrepreneurs. Their dedication to uplifting the Black community and contributing to the betterment of society has paved the way for future generations. We stand on the shoulders of those who came before us, and it is our duty to continue their legacy of service.

Being in service isn't about sacrificing yourself or your well-being. It's about finding ways to use your strengths and passions to make a positive difference. When we serve, we honor not only ourselves but the ancestors who fought for our freedom and the future generations who will benefit from our contributions.

As Black men and women, our responsibility to serve is not just an obligation—it is a privilege. Every day, we have the opportunity to share our unique gifts with the world and make a meaningful impact on the lives of others. By embracing the spirit of service, we fulfill the deeper purpose of our existence and contribute to a brighter, more inclusive future for all.

As Muhammad Ali so eloquently stated, "Being in service is the rent we pay for our time here on earth." Let us continue to pay that rent with love, dedication, and the unwavering commitment to making the world a better place.

Public Enemy's powerful anthem, "Don't Believe the Hype," was more than just a song—it was a declaration of independence from the negative narratives constantly projected onto Black people. The message was clear: do not fall for the lies, distortions, and stereotypes perpetuated by the media. Instead, recognize your own power, truth, and potential. In a world where the media often sensationalizes and distorts the image of Black men and women, the wisdom of that message is more relevant than ever.

We live in an era where Black excellence is undeniable. From the boardrooms to the classrooms, from the world of entertainment to the halls of government, Black people are thriving like never before. Despite the overwhelming evidence of success, the media frequently highlights stories that reinforce negative stereotypes, portraying Black communities as broken, divided, or in constant struggle. But let me be clear: those images are not the reality of who we are. The truth is that we have made, and continue to make, incredible progress.

For decades, mainstream media has been complicit in shaping a distorted image of Black people. News outlets and entertainment industries have often focused disproportionately on crime, poverty, and dysfunction within Black communities. This narrative feeds into harmful stereotypes that make it seem as though Black people are somehow less capable of success or happiness. But nothing could be further from the truth.

While it's essential to acknowledge the challenges our community faces, we must not let those obstacles define us. Yes, systemic racism exists. Yes, there are injustices that must be confronted. But these issues should never overshadow the incredible achievements and progress we've made. For every negative story the media pushes, there are countless examples of Black people excelling in all areas of life. We have broken barriers, shattered glass ceilings, and proven time and again that our potential is limitless.

Representation matters. Seeing yourself reflected in positive, powerful roles can change your entire outlook on life. That's why it's so important to seek out stories that uplift and inspire. Look to the Black leaders, innovators, and trailblazers who are paving the way for future generations. From Kamala Harris becoming the first Black woman Vice President, to entrepreneurs building multi-million-dollar businesses, to everyday heroes making a difference in their communities—these are the stories that show who we truly are.

The success of Black men and women is not an anomaly—it is part of a long history of resilience, brilliance, and excellence. It is time we control our own narrative, elevating stories that highlight our strengths, achievements, and contributions. We must remind ourselves, and each other, that we are far more than what the media portrays.

The story of Black people in America is one of progress. We have gone from being enslaved to becoming leaders in every sector of society. From civil rights to political power, from culture-shaping movements to financial empowerment, our strides are undeniable. The future is even brighter.

The numbers tell a different story than what you often see in the media. Black businesses are growing at unprecedented rates, particularly those owned by Black women, who are the fastest-growing group of entrepreneurs in the country. More Black students are earning college degrees, and more Black professionals are entering fields traditionally dominated by others. The rise of Black voices in politics, education, technology, and the arts reflects the undeniable reality that we are shaping the future of America.

It's easy to get discouraged when bombarded with negative portrayals of our community. But here's the truth: you have the power to choose what you believe and what you focus on. Don't believe the hype. Instead, believe in yourself, your community, and the incredible potential within you.

Black men and women have always been innovators, creators, and leaders. We have always found ways to rise above adversity and thrive, no matter the circumstances. Now, more than ever, we are poised to continue that legacy of greatness. This is a time of empowerment, opportunity, and growth. It is a time to celebrate how far we've come and to look forward with optimism about where we are going.

As we continue to make strides in education, business, politics, and culture, it's clear that the future for Black people in America is filled with possibility. We have the power to shape our destinies, to define our narratives, and to uplift one another as we forge ahead. The next generation of Black leaders is already making waves, and their impact will be felt across the world.

We must continue to push back against the negative images and embrace the truth: we are powerful, we are brilliant, and we are capable of achieving anything we set our minds to. The progress we have made is just the beginning. The future is filled with even more success, growth, and achievement.

Public Enemy's call to "Don't Believe the Hype" was a rallying cry for Black people to reject the negativity and embrace the truth of our greatness. We cannot allow the media to dictate how we see ourselves. We must take control of our narrative, celebrate our progress, and continue to strive for excellence.

The story of Black people in America is one of triumph, resilience, and endless potential. We are not defined by the challenges we face, but by the victories we achieve. The future is bright, and Black men and women will continue to rise, thrive, and lead. So, don't believe the hype. Believe in the promise of who we are and the incredible future that lies ahead.

About Coach Michael Taylor

Michael Taylor is a shining example of resilience and determination, having overcome immense personal challenges to become a renowned life coach, motivational speaker, and bestselling author. His unwavering commitment to empowering others has inspired countless individuals to pursue their dreams and live extraordinary lives.

A former high school dropout, Michael faced seemingly insurmountable obstacles, including divorce, bankruptcy, foreclosure, depression, and even homelessness. Yet, through sheer grit and an unshakable belief in himself, he emerged from these trials as a beacon of hope and inspiration.

With 16 published books under his belt (primarily dealing with the changing roles of manhood and masculinity), Michael's words have touched the lives of readers worldwide, guiding them towards personal growth, self-discovery, and the realization of their full potential. As a certified life coach, he has dedicated his life to helping men and women break free from self-imposed limitations and embrace the extraordinary within themselves.

Michael's journey has been a testament to the power of perseverance and the indomitable human spirit. As the president and CEO of Creation Publishing Group, he continues to champion the pursuit of dreams and the creation of a life filled with purpose and fulfillment.

With an infectious optimism and an unwavering passion for the impossible, Michael Taylor stands as a testament to the boundless potential that lies within each of us. He firmly believes that there has never been a better time to be alive on this planet, and his mission is to inspire others to embrace this belief and live their lives to the fullest.

Resources

www.coachmichaeltaylor.com

www.sistahsummit.com

www.shatterthestereotypes.com

www.jesuswasacoach.com

www.joypassionprofit.com

Here is the list of the amazing women who contributed to the Brotha To Sistah Empowerment Summit and provided insights and wisdom to this book. Be sure to check them out and follow them on social media.
Jewel Diamond Taylor – Black Women Empowerment and Transformation
www.jeweldiamondtaylor.com

Janine Ingram – The Power of Self Love
www.janineaingram.com

Anita Charlot – The Grown Ass Woman Philosophy
www.anitacharlot.com

Anitra Rice – Understanding and Healing From Grief and Loss
www.thefolfoundation.org

Dr. Audrey Dawson – Keys To Building A Healthy Blended Family
ahinds2014@gmail.com

Dr. Candace Canady – Your Body Is Your Temple
www.coupleofchiros.com

Franka Baly – Are You Ready To Become An Entrepreneur?
www.fbuxconsulting.com

Dr. Omai Kofi – Get Your Mind Right To Get Your Money Right
www.meetdro.com

Dr. Pam Perry – Building A Powerful Brand Identity
www.pamperrypr.com

Rev. Bernette Jones – Developing True Connection With The Divine
www.consciousnessagency.com